WIN
FIXED-ODDS
BETTING

WIN AT
FIXED-ODDS FOOTBALL BETTING

by

MALCOLM BOYLE

OLDCASTLE BOOKS

1993

Oldcastle Books

134 Southdown Road

Harpenden, Herts, AL5 1PU

Copyright © Malcolm Boyle 1993

First publication

The right of Malcolm Boyle to be identified as author of this work has been asserted by him in accordance with the Copyright, Designs & Patents Act, 1988.

A CIP catalogue record for this book is available from the British Library.

ISBN 1-874061-18-1   Win at Fixed Odds Football Betting

9 8 7 6 5 4 3 2 1

Typeset in Century Schoolbook by Koinonia Ltd, Manchester.
Printed and bound by Guernsey Press.

Contents

FIXED ODDS FOOTBALL BETTING

The Newsletter

FREE TRIAL OFFER

Although the material found in Win at Fixed Odds Football Betting has proven invaluable to users during the early part of the season it is important that you keep abreast of all the latest trends to maximise your potential profits. For instance did you know that we said that Norwich were the team to back to win 3-2 away from home - they won their first away match of the season 3-2 - *at odds of 100/1!*

More early season information that would have netted a tidy profit included:

- Rotherham's had a habit of 3-3 draws last year. First match of season drawn 3-3 at odds of 66/1!

- Leave Everton out of Pools selections we advised - 10 matches into the season and still no draws!

- Look for Darlington to be involved in jackpot draws we suggested - Darlington drew 3 of their first 5 matches 1-1!

- Man Utd consistently won 3-0 at home last season - in no time at all they won 3-0 twice at home this season!

- Teddy Sheringham was clearly superior to his colleagues in the first goal department in the 92/93 season - He scored the first goal of the game in Spurs first match of the season!

Convinced you need our newsletter? We are so sure that you will want the information we can provide that we will send you an up to date sample newsletter at ABSOLUTELY NO COST! When you choose to subscribe the rates are £10 for a single fortnightly issue, £25 for 4 issues and £69 for 13 issues. Cheques or P.O.'s should be payable to Oldcastle Books Ltd - we accept Access, Visa or Switch.

Please send your address details on a separate piece of paper to *Fixed Odds Newsletter, Oldcastle Books, 18 Coleswood Rd, Harpenden, Herts, AL5 1EQ* and we will send you the current newsletter by return post - Free of charge.

Introduction

Each time you pick up a fixed odds football coupon, you probably do so with supreme confidence. After all, you only have three possibilities to choose from in each match, so what could be easier?

Naturally the bookmaker has the staking rules as he would like them, but compared to a thirty runner handicap at Goodwood, you must fancy your chances.

Why is it then that week after week you curse your luck when, once again, one team has let you down for a treble or an accumulator.

Whatever the reason, this book will endeavour to help bring about the downfall of the bookmaker.

We hope to persuade you to take the fixed odds coupon more seriously, and show you that there are methods which will help you to win money on a regular basis.

We do not claim that it will be easy, but the knowledge you will gain from this book will undoubtedly help.

The form book in football can be misleading of course. It does not follow that if Bolton beat Stoke, and because Stoke beat West Brom, that Bolton will necessarily beat West Brom. Even if they do, you will still have to find another four bankers if you include a home win with most bookmakers.

However, you have to be positive, and we are sure that you will fare better this season than you did the last time around if you read this book.

In future, you will also be able to obtain a regular newsletter throughout the season. (See details at back of book.)

The information in the newsletter includes updated facts and figures which are in this issue, as well as an exclusive pricing comparison study.

We will list all the forthcoming league games alongside the results and prices of last season's corresponding fixture. Therefore you will be able to determine genuine value based on the results as they were priced last year.

As an example we could use Arsenal versus Manchester City at Highbury. 'The Gunners' started at 8/11 and duly obliged, and

1

therefore you could take the opinion that if Arsenal start at 8/11 or better this season you should use them as one of your bankers. Obviously form changes from year to year but this service could prove invaluable in the months ahead. With respect to such clubs, it will certainly assist you with the likes of Lincoln versus Gillingham during the depths of winter.

Sports betting has come on in leaps and bounds over the last ten years or so, with football betting dominating the market.

Even Trevor 'sit on the fence' Brooking has a bet on the fixed odds coupon, so you are in good company if you enjoy a wager.

Trevor admitted last season that his best effort was eight winning teams from ten selections. If you read Win at ... Fixed Odds Football Trevor, you might just hit the jackpot!

Points to note

All the information in this book pertains to league matches only. We may refer to beaten favourites from time to time. For the purpose of this book, we actually mean that the favourite did not win. They may have drawn the match in question, but to the punter the important matter is that their money is lost, thus we refer to them as beaten favourites.

The odds that are published have all been taken from one of the major bookmakers. This is for consistancy reasons. Odds will vary from layer to layer over the course of a season, but the differences will even out generally.

Don't leave betting to chance

Pricing up matches yourself

My general criticism of the average fixed odds football punter, is that he doesn't take the coupon seriously.

Nine times out of ten, clients will sift through their horse bets on a Saturday morning, and then see what spare change they have to invest on the football coupon.

Obviously there are those amongst you that put a lot of work into their selections but you are few and far between.

This of course is very much how the bookmaker would like it to be. They want you to look down the lists and settle for an unlikely looking accumulator which requires five selections or more.

The coupons themselves are marketed especially to encourage you to put more selections down than you intend.

The bookmakers advertise wonderful winning opportunities, stating that the minimum odds for nine or ten homes are 20/1 and 33/1 or whatever the case might be.

The short list, the sections and mini-sections offer incredible returns and are promoted on the coupons as offering you odds of up to thirty thousand to one or more.

It is understandable therefore, that punters will be sucked in by such marketing and advertising techniques. Punters generally cannot be bothered to wade through the formlines and hence give themselves little chance of success on the coupon.

They will be drawn into betting on the sections list and the like, which were invented by the bookmaker, for the bookmaker. The more selections you make, the less chance you have of winning.

The bookmaker cannot really lose when you think about it. Even when they lay substantial winning bets, the public relations people take over and market the successful wager to such a degree that turnover the following week goes through the roof.

The question is then, how can you beat the bookmaker, or at least oppose him on level terms?

There are various ways that you can help your own cause.

The golden rule is that you don't leave betting to chance.

Obviously you can spend hour upon hour going through results to keep yourself fully up to date, which at least gives you the professional footing that the odds compilers seek to achieve.

You can also look for assistance from the trade newspapers. Sport coverage, and football betting in particular, has improved dramatically over the last two or three years. The statistics and information that can now be found can only help in your quest to defeat the enemy.

Unfortunately though, too many people adopt a sloppy attitude to fixed odds betting.

It is amazing just how many people allow themselves to be dictated to by the bookmakers.

They will breeze through the fixed odds coupon and scrawl down a few selections, which are usually short priced home 'bankers'. Punters will take the odds compilers opinion whether the home side is a good thing, and then expect to pick out four others to make up a winning accumulator.

What can the punter do to ensure that he is getting value?

The best way to choose your selections is for you to compile your own prices, and then compare them to the coupons. This way you can see for yourself where the real value lies in fixed odds betting.

How do I as a punter go about making prices if I haven't a clue where to start?

This exercise is nowhere near as difficult as you might imagine ... and to make it easier for you, I have printed a table which concentrates on the prices of the draw in any match you might like to price up. [see pages 6-7]

Your first job is to evaluate the price of the draw in the match in question. Then you simply look down the table to see what prices are available to you for the home and away sides.

Use logic and latest results to influence your price of the draw. If the two sides are pretty evenly matched and have a habit of playing in drawn games, you will be looking towards the 2/1 area [i.e. a 33% chance] for the stalemate. A good example at the end of last year might have been Sheffield Wednesday v Arsenal. On the other hand, if you were looking to price up Rangers against Motherwell you should be looking at the 13/5 category [i.e. a 28% chance] or thereabouts for the draw.

There may not seem that much difference in the prices to you initially, but this exercise will eventually teach you just how important these fractions are.

Take the 2/1 price for the draw as an example.

If you were looking at the Wednesday/Arsenal fixture and had decided on 2/1 the draw, how would you bet on the home and away side?

Look down the table and decide which of the pairs of prices suit best.

I would be inclined to take a view of laying 11/8 Wednesday and 9/5 Arsenal.

Just to convince yourself that your prices are correct, look at the fractions of the prices as they stand. I am saying that Wednesday would win 8 matches from every 19 between the teams at Hillsborough. By the same token, I estimate that Arsenal would win 5 from every 14.

So whichever prices you select, simply turn them around as I have done here, and you will be giving yourself a guarantee that the odds are not a million miles away from being accurate, just as accurate in fact as the professional odds compilers.

Draw prices

Simply choose the price of the draw for the match in question, and then look down the relevant table to see which pairs of prices are available for the two teams.

15/8		2/1		11/5		9/4	
13/8	13/8	6/4	13/8	6/4	6/4	11/8	13/8
8/5	8/5	11/8	9/5	13/8	11/8	5/4	7/4
6/4	7/4	5/4	2/1	5/4	9/5	6/5	15/8
11/8	15/8	6/5	11/5	6/5	15/8	11/10	2/1
5/4	85/40	11/10	11/5	11/10	2/1	1/1	9/4
6/5	9/4	1/1	13/5	1/1	11/5	10/11	13/5
11/10	5/2	10/11	3/1	10/11	13/5	5/6	11/4
		5/6	10/3	5/6	11/4	4/5	3/1
		4/5	7/2	4/5	3/1	8/11	10/3
		8/11	4/1	8/11	7/2	4/6	7/2
		4/6	9/2	4/6	4/1	8/13	4/1
		8/13	5/1	8/13	9/2	4/7	5/1
		4/7	6/1			8/15	11/2
						1/2	6/1

	12/5		5/2		13/5
5/4	13/8	4/5	5/2	4/6	3/1
11/10	15/8	8/11	3/1	8/13	7/2
1/1	2/1	4/6	10/3	4/7	4/1
5/6	13/5	8/13	7/2	1/2	5/1
5/6	12/5	4/7	4/1	4/9	6/1
4/5	11/4	8/15	9/2	2/5	7/1
8/11	3/1	1/2	5/1		
4/6	7/2*	4/11	9/1		
4/6	10/3*				
8/13	4/1				
4/7	9/2				
8/15	5/1				
1 /2	11/2				

*If you look at the 12/5 table and read down to the pairings of prices 4/6–7/2 & 4/6–10/3, you may feel that I have erred. What you will find however when you study the prices on the coupons in the shops, is that the bookmakers tend to look for more potential profit from the Scottish matches, particularly the first and second division games. Therefore the prices on offer to the public will sometimes be 'tighter'.

Ante-post betting

**Beware of betting on football cup competitions –
Are you backing favourites or outsiders?**

Here are some examples of the actual price you are taking per
round when you bet ante-post on cup football:
Betting before the third round of the F.A.Cup (last 64)

Price to win outright	Actual odds to win through each round
13/2	(2/5)
8	(4/9)
10	(1/2)
12	(8/15)
16	(8/13)
20	(4/6)
25	(8/11)
33	(4/5)
40	(5/6)
50	(10/11)
66	(Evs)
100	(6/5)
200	(11/8)

Whilst 25/1 might look attractive about your fancy, it becomes
very poor value when you break down the odds in this manner.
25/1 to most people would represent an outsider in terms of
winning the competition. When you analyse the odds though,
you realise that these outsiders of yours are actually 8/11
favourites to win every one of the six rounds they must win if they
are to lift the trophy. Are they favourites or outsiders?
Before the fourth round of the competition (last 32) the bookmakers might bet like this:

5 (4/9)	12 (4/6)	33 (21/20)	
6 (1/2)	16 (4/5)	40 (11/10)	
8 (4/7)	20 (5/6)	50 (6/5)	100 (6/4)

Once again the figures in the brackets represent the true price of the team to win each round if they are to win the tournament. Fifth round betting could look like this (last 16)

10/3 (4/9)	8 (8/11)
4 (1/2)	10 (4/5)
5 (4/7)	12 (10/11)
6 (8/13)	16 (21/20)
7 (4/6)	20 (11/10)

Prices on offer for the sixth round (last 8) could look like this:

9/4 (1/2)	6 (10/11)
11/4 (4/7)	8 (11/10)
10/3 (8/13)	10 (5/4)
4 (8/11)	14 (6/4)
9/2 (4/5)	16 (13/8)
	20 (7/4)

Suddenly ante-post betting on the F.A.Cup and the like loses its attraction.

How do you know that these prices I have quoted are correct? On the next page you will find a table of figures. There is a decimal figure to feed into a simple calculator which represents the price alongside.

Remember how many rounds a team must win if it is to win the tournament.

Third round	(last 64)	6 matches
Fourth round	(last 32)	5 matches
Fifth round	(last 16)	4 matches
Sixth round	(last 8)	3 matches

So if you are at the fifth round stage of the cup, your team needs to win through another four matches.

If you consider your team to be 8/13 chances against [62%] the average other teams left in the competition, you need to multiply 1.615 by the same figure four times. That should give you an answer of around 6/1. If your team is 13/2 or more, by all means have your bet, if they are less than 6/1, keep the money in your pocket.

Price (Decimal) Table

1/8	1.125	Evs	2.0	4/1	5.0
2/15	1.133	11/10	2.10	9/2	5.5
1/7	1.143	6/5	2.2	5/1	6.0
2/13	1.154	5/4	2.25	11/2	6.5
1/6	1.167	11/8	2.375	6/1	7.0
2/11	1.182	6/4	2.5	13/2	7.5
1/5	1.20	8/5	2.60	7/1	8.0
2/9	1.222	13/8	2.625	15/2	8.5
1/4	1.25	7/4	2.75	8/1	9.0
2/7	1.286	9/5	2.80	17/2	9.5
3/10	1.30	15/8	2.875	9/1	10.0
1/3	1.333	2/1	3.0	10/1	11.0
4/11	1.363	85/40	3.125	12/1	13.0
2/5	1.40	11/5	3.20	14/1	15.0
4/9	1.444	9/4	3.25	16/1	17.0
1/2	1.50	12/5	3.40	18/1	19.0
8/15	1.533	5/2	3.5	20/1	21.0
4/7	1.571	13/5	3.60	22/1	23.0
8/13	1.615	11/4	3.75	25/1	26.0
4/6	1.667	14/5	3.80	28/1	29.0
8/11	1.727	3/1	4.0	33/1	34.0
4/5	1.80	10/3	4.333	50/1	51.0
5/6	1.833	7/2	4.5	66/1	67.0
10/11	1.909	18/5	4.60	100/1	101.0

This table can also be used to work out your winning bets. Suppose you have a line of five homes up with the 'awkward' prices of:

8/13   11/8   10/3   11/10   6/5

Simply multiply the prices by their decimal figures:
1.615 x 2.375 x 4.333 x 2.1 x 2.2 to give you a reading of 76·78
Finally take this figure and multiply it by your stake i.e. If your stake was 25p, multiply 76.78 by .25 to give you £19.19
Or if your stake was £5.00, multiply 76.78 by 5.00 to give you £383.90
You can use this table for all your win bets in future, whether it be for football, greyhounds or horses.

When is a favourite not a favourite? (even when it is sometimes odds on)

The simple answer is in football matches.
People actually presume that the shortest price chalked up between a home team, an away team and the draw is the true and proper favourite. Not so!
Unless a team is priced at 8/11 or shorter, they are not favourites for that particular match.
When a team starts at 10/11 for example, you will find that the percentages added together for the other two possibilities will outweigh that of the 10/11 chance. Therefore the favourite for the match in question is for the 10/11 side NOT to win.
These peculiarities come about because of the way bookmakers bet on football matches. They are betting to around eleven per cent margins in single match terms, and therefore the balance of the percentages becomes tilted.
Remember next time you are filling in your fixed odds coupons that unless one of your 'bankers' is 8/11 or shorter, it is not even favourite for the fixture. They are the 'favourites' in terms of being the shortest price on offer about the three possibilities of result, but the true favourite in relation to the match is that they will NOT win.

Professional betting

Successful staking plans

What do we mean by professional betting and are there people around who actually make a living out of gambling on the fixed odds coupons?

In truth, there would be very few people who would be earning a living from football betting.

There are however, hundreds of people who make their gambling pay. They could not be described as professional punters for reasons I will give in a moment.

The professional man who seeks to raise money from gambling will have a 'tunnel vision' approach to his methods of betting. He will stick rigidly to the rules that he has set for himself, and he will not be sidetracked by anything the market has to offer.

He generally will not bet on handicap races, and he will eliminate chance wherever possible.

He will take into account the racecourse, the going, the form and the draw. Then he will look into the annual and current statistics of the trainer and the jockey, and then weigh up the opposition. Eventually, he will evaluate a price which he believes would be worth a wager. If the bookmaker offers those odds, or maybe a higher price then, and only then, will our professional punter have a bet – invariably 'tax free' on course.

Taking all this into account, we cannot honestly say that a professional punter exists in football betting.

He can't very well ring Kenny Dalgleish and ask if it is raining in Blackburn! He cannot determine whether Alan Shearer will 'need the run.' He simply cannot easily get inside the football business on a day to day basis.

No, the professional person we are talking about is one who looks to repetitive occurences within football. We would like to think he would view this book as an informed guide to help him win on a regular basis.

The person we are describing, would not walk into a shop and pick up a coupon if it happens to be in his line of vision. We are looking for him (or her) to view each betting day as a valuable gambling opportunity, provided he (or she) has done their homework.

When I worked as an odds compiler at the headquarters of one of our largest bookmakers, I saw the difference between 'professional' clients and those people who had a wager almost for the sake of having a bet.

The 'professional' punter stood out principally through his staking plan.

In those days, the 2-1 scoreline was particularly repetitive as a result, and the 'professional' people latched onto the fact.

These people would seek out around eight matches on the coupon, and then perm up the 2-1 scoreline in doubles and trebles. These bets would be wagered at very heavy stakes, which they would repeat from week to week.

The very fact that they were looking for more than one result, makes it impossible for them to be described as professional.

They were however, very professional in their outlook and in their attitude to betting. They had determined the correct scoreline, and all that remained was to choose the appropriate teams.

The chance they took (as opposed to our professional punter), was that two or more results would 'click' on the same day. I can assure you that these people were successful on several occasions.

As further proof of their professionalism, they would continue this method of betting until it became successful. Obviously not everyone has 'bottomless pockets', so you must bet to your means at all times if you fancy giving this type of gambling a try.

If you follow this method of betting, I maintain you have your best opportunity of winning money on the fixed odds coupons.

Take a look at last season as an example.

Admittedly we are looking at bets after knowing the results, but there are reasons why we are centering our attentions on the following bets which I will explain afterwards.

If you look at the opening day of the season, you will find that four matches in the Premier Division ended as 1-1 draws.

Your stake plan could have been 165 10p trebles and 330 1p four-team accumulators. [You will understand from the staking plan that there were eleven Premier matches that weekend.]

The return would have been around £127.69 for a stake of £19.80 plus tax.

You would have multiplied your stake six and a half times before tax deductions.

There were four more 1-1 draws on the weekend of December the 19th, and countless numbers of coupons that offered two draws and upwards.

If we take a look at the First Division we will find five matches that ended 0-0 on the 29th August.

There were twelve matches that weekend, so our stake could have been 220 5p trebles and 495 1p fourfolds - £15.95 plus tax. You will realise I hope, that we are not getting carried away with hefty stakes here. We appreciate that people have a budget, and we are being realistic.

Getting back to the 0-0 draws, your return would have been over £717.00.

Another match in the division ended 1-0 and if, yes it is a big word we know, if that match had ended without a goal your return would have been well over eighteen hundred pounds. And all this for comparitively small stakes.

Once again there were several weeks where the 0-0 draw was a repetitive result.

We single these correct scores out for logical reasons.

The Premier Division produced the largest number of jackpot draws, and the First Division gave more 0-0 scorelines than any other. It is simply a case of keeping your eyes open. Alternatively there is our weekly newsletter which will keep you completely informed, during the current season.

Without going into too much detail, the 1-3 scoreline in Scottish matches has been reasonably repetitive.

On the 23rd of January for example, there were only seven matches played north of the border, and two of those games finished at 1-3. The odds for the correct score double was 1,325-1. You must appreciate as well that very often, as in this case, there are several non runners to boost your potential returns due to postponements.

Correct score betting offers tremendous potential if used in the correct manner. Compare the facts above to those that follow, and I think you will agree with me that permutation correct score betting is worth a gamble.

On the 30th of January, the Second Division threw up some miserable results for potential fixed odds punters.

Just one favourite obliged and ten were beaten. The winning team was odds on, but they were the only winners from six odds on chances.

If you added the results of the top three English leagues together that day, they read as follows:-

  7 winning favourites.

25 beaten favourites (i.e. favourites that did not win)

  6 winning odds on favourites.

10 beaten odds on favourites.

This pattern is generally the rule and not the exception, though granted the example is extreme.

On the 3rd April, the English Premier produced seven winning favourites out of eight. Unfortunately, if you permed some of these teams with favourites from other leagues as is the norm, you would probably have lost.

On the remainder of the coupon, there were seventeen winning favourites and twenty-nine that were unsuccessful.

On the 17th of October, the Scottish Premier produced six winning favourites from six games. Elsewhere in Scotland though the sequence broke down badly. The second division for example produced just one winning favourite with six beaten.

The first three Saturday's of the season produced a total of just nine winning favourites in the Premier League in England. There were nineteen beaten favourites. In this time there were just two odds on winners, with eight odds on 'bankers' failing to win.

And that is generally the rule I am afraid. Everyone can pick winners, but can they pick the required number on the coupons? Whilst we have generally approved of correct score betting in principle, we have to acknowledge that punters get carried away with potential scorelines.

My own advice for starters is to steer clear of investing in matches that involve your own club. The majority of us have a favourite team, even if we do not necessarily go to support them very often. For betting purposes we should avoid including such teams unless they are genuinely producing repetitive scorelines. What often occurs unfortunatly, is that we contrive to put our teams forward to score umpteen goals, when the norm is totally the opposite. The bookmakers rub their hands with joy as punter after punter comes steaming in expecting his team to score a hatful of goals. Have you been one of those punters?

15

I would wager that you would have lost money betting on Manchester United last year. Yes they had a great season, but as an example can you tell me how many times they scored four goals or more?

On the following pages you will find each team listed alongside the number of times they scored a minimum of four gaols. The figures in brackets are the number of occasions that they scored four or more away from home.

It is my belief that the statistics will surprise you, and if you learn nothing else from this book, you should at least bring your correct score predictions into the realms of realism!

Team scoring performances

The number of times teams scored four or more goals last year.

PREMIER LEAGUE		FIRST DIVISION	
Arsenal	1	Barnsley	2 (2)
Aston Villa	2	Birmingham	1
Blackburn	3	Bristol City	2 (1)
Chelsea	2	Charlton	1
Coventry	2 (1)	Derby	2 (1)
Everton	1 (1)	Grimsby	2 (1)
Ipswich	1	Leicester	3
Leeds	2	Luton	0
Liverpool	5	Millwall	5
Man. City	2 (1)	Notts Cnty	2
Man. Utd.	2	Oxford	3
Norwich	3 (1)	Peterborough	1
Oldham	5	Portsmouth	7 (3)
Q.P.R.	4 (1)	Southend	2 (1)
Sheff. Utd.	2	Sunderland	1
Sheff. Wed.	1	Tranmere	3
Southamton	1	Watford	1
Tottenham	4	Wolves	3 (1)
Wimbledon	2		

The number of times teams scored four or more goals last year.

SECOND DIVISION		THIRD DIVISION	
Blackpool	1	Bury	2 (1)
Bournemouth	2	Carlisle	1
Bradford City	2 (1)	Chesterfield	2 (1)
Brighton	0	Colchester	2 (1)
Burnley	2	Crewe	5
Exeter	0	Darlington	1
Fulham	1	Doncaster	1
Hartlepool	0	Gillingham	2
Huddersfield	1	Hereford	0
Hull	1	Lincoln	1
Leyton Orient	7 (1)	Northampton	1
Plymouth	2 (1)	Rochdale	5 (2)
Port Vale	5 (3)	Scarborough	4 (1)
Reading	2	Scunthorpe	3
Rotherham	1	Shrewsbury	3 (1)
Stockport	6 (2)	Torquay	1 (1)
Swansea	2	Walsall	3 (2)

The number of times teams scored four or more goals last year.

SCOTTISH PREMIER		SCOTTISH FIRST		SCOTTISH SECOND	
Aberdeen	5 (3)	Ayr	1	Albion	1
Celtic	3 (1)	Clydebank	4	Alloa	3 (2)
Dundee	2 (1)	Dumbarton	2	Arbroath	2
Dundee Utd.	3 (3)	Dunfermline	3 (2)	Berwick	1
Hearts	0	Hamilton	1 (2)	East Fife	4 (2)
Hibernian	0	Morton	2	East Stirl'g	4 (2)
Motherwell	0	Stirling	1	Forfar	7 (1)
Rangers	9 (6)	St. Mirren	2	Montrose	3 (1)
St. Johnstone	1			Q.O.T. South	3 (2)
Partick	0			Queen's Park	2
				Stenhs'muir	2 (2)
				Stranraer	5 (3)

Odds on favourites

According to my records, there were 741 winning odds on favourites from 1,329 last year.

This evaluates to a percentage figure of 55.7%. In betting terms, this means that every odds on favourite that played in the leagues last year were actually 4/5 to win in reality.

Our figures confirm that the Scottish Premier led the way in winners, just in front of the First division north of the border.

The only league to record a percentage below fifty was the English Third Division.

For the record here is how the leagues fared:

1.	Scottish Premier	61.6%
2.	Scottish First	61.4
3.	Second Division	58.6
4.	First Division	57.0
5.	Premier Division	52.1
6.	Scottish Second	51.5
7.	Third Division	48.5

On the following pages you will find divisional lists of teams with their odds on performances last season. Teams that have been promoted or relegated have not been included.

Record of Teams starting at odds-on

PREMIER LEAGUE

Arsenal	7-14	50.0%
Aston Villa	10-16	62.5
Blackburn	8-15	53.3
Chelsea	3-8	37.5
Coventry	1-6	16.7
Everton	2-7	28.6
Ipswich	1-5	20.0
Leeds	8-14	57.1
Liverpool	10-14	71.4
Manchester City	4-11	36.4
Manchester United	13-19	68.4
	2-3 away *	66.7
Norwich	8-13	61.5
Oldham	1-2	50.0
Q.P.R.	3-6	50.0
Sheffield United	3-5	60.0
Sheffield United	5-12	41.7
Southampton	2-4	50.0
Tottenham	3-6	50.0
Wimbledon	1-1	100.0

*Manchester United were the only team who started odds on away from home

Record of Teams starting at odds-on

FIRST DIVISION

Barnsley	4-6	66.7%
Birmingham	4-4	100.0
Bristol City	3-6	50.0
Charlton	6-14	42.8
Derby	6-17	35.3
Grimsby	4-7	57.1
Leicester	10-17	58.8
Luton	1-5	20.0
Millwall	9-16	56.2
Notts County	2-4	50.0
Oxford	2-5	40.0
Peterborough	4-10	40.0
Portsmouth	14-17	82.3
Southend	2-2	100.0
Sunderland	2-8	25.0
Tranmere	10-15	66.7
Watford	1-2	50.0
Wolves	6-14	42.9

AWAY FROM HOME

Derby	1-1	100.0
Leicester	0-1	—
Millwall	0-1	—

Record of Teams starting at odds-on

SECOND DIVISION

Blackpool	3-6	50.0%
Bournemouth	3-9	33.3
Bradford	7-15	46.7
Brighton	9-16	56.2
Burnley	7-13	53.8
Exeter	3-7	42.9
Fulham	5-9	55.5
Hartlepool	3-8	37.5
Huddersfield	2-4	50.0
Hull	5-10	50.0
Leyton Orient	10-16	64.7
Plymouth	8-12	66.7
Port Vale	9-15	60.0
Reading	6-9	66.7
Rotherham	6-16	37.5
Stockport	6-16	37.5
Swansea	11-17	64.7

AWAY FROM HOME

Fulham	1-1	100.0
Port Vale	3-4	75.0

Record of Teams starting at odds-on

THIRD DIVISION

Bury	5-12	41.7%
Carlisle	2-3	66.7
Chesterfield	4-9	44.4
Colchester	8-10	80.0
Crewe	11-17	64.7
Darlington	1-4	25.0
Doncaster	1-5	20.0
Gillingham	1-2	50.0
Hereford	0-1	—
Lincoln	6-14	42.8
Northampton	0-4	—
Rochdale	3-9	33.3
Scarborough	3-11	27.3
Scunthorpe	4-9	44.4
Shrewsbury	5-13	38.5
Torquay	1-3	33.3
Walsall	8-16	50.0

AWAY FROM HOME

Colchester	0-1	—

Record of Teams starting at odds-on

SCOTTISH PREMIER

Team	Record	Percentage
Aberdeen	11-18	61.1%
Celtic	11-18	61.1
Dundee	3-4	75.0
Dundee United	8-14	57.1
Hearts	9-15	60.0
Hibernian	4-10	40.0
Motherwell	1-4	25.0
Partick	0-4	—
Rangers	20-21!	95.2!
St. Johnstone	4-7	57.1

AWAY FROM HOME

Team	Record	Percentage
Aberdeen	6-7	85.7
Celtic	3-6	50.0
Rangers	9-14	64.3

Record of Teams starting at odds-on

SCOTTISH FIRST DIVISION

Ayr	3-7	42.8%
Clydebank	5-9	55.5
Dumbarton	1-4	25.0
Dunfermline	7-16	43.7
Hamilton	9-13	69.2
Morton	9-11	81.8
Stirling	1-2	50.0
St. Mirren	7-13	53.8

AWAY FROM HOME

Ayr	1-2	50.0
Clydebank	1-1	100.0
Dunfermline	2-3	66.7
Hamilton	2-3	66.7
Morton	2-2	100.0
St. Mirren	3-4	75.0

Record of Teams starting at odds-on

SCOTTISH SECOND DIVISION

Albion	NIL	
Alloa	7-14	50.0%
Arbroath	4-7	57.1
Berwick	3-7	42.8
East Fife	3-8	37.5
East Stirling	0-2	—
Forfar	10-17	58.8
Montrose	3-9	33.3
Queen of the South	1-4	25.0
Queen's Park	0-1	—
Stenhousemuir	3-7	42.8
Stranraer	5-13	38.5

AWAY FROM HOME

Arbroath	1-2	50.0
East Fife	0-1	—
Forfar	1-2	50.0
Stenhousemuir	2-2	100.0

Odds against

Although this book has a tendancy to direct you away from basic team selection betting, we fully appreciate that you are not going to change your habits overnight.

There have been wonderful stories over the years of people who have made small fortunes from successful accumulators. Long may that trend continue.

I write this as a prelude to the odds against chapter for a specific reason.

If you indulge in these speculative accumulators, I implore you to concentrate on the teams at decent odds. As a former betting shop manager, I assure you that coupons that come into an office with the emphasis on odds on selections hold no fear for the bookmaker whatsoever.

The punter who looks to odds on chances invariably beats himself through greed. He is forever looking for one more team to boost his accumulator. The odds on punter will even have his bet worked out before he puts it on,if he is able to calculate the returns.

No, the really impressive wins that have been made, have been made up by a smaller numbers of odds against winners.

The emphasis should be on small stakes generally though, as the majority of your spare cash could be put to better use for reasons already given.

Hopefully the figures on the following pages will help you to find that elusive winning accumulator.

The figures in brackets denote the home statistics.

Performance level at even money or odds against

PREMIER DIVISION

Arsenal	8-28	(1-7)
Aston Villa	11-26	(3-5)
Blackburn	12-27	(5-6)
Chelsea	11-34	(6-13)
Coventry	12-36	(6-15)
Everton	13-35	(5-14)
Ipswich	11-37	(7-16)
Leeds	4-28	(4-7)
Liverpool	6-28	(3-7)
Manchester City	11-31	(3-10)
Manchester Utd.	9-20	(1-2)
Norwich	13-29	(5-8)
Oldham	12-40	(9-19)
Q.P.R.	14-36	(8-15)
Sheffield Utd.	11-37	(7-16)
Sheffield Wed.	10-30	(4-9)
Southampton	11-38	(8-17)
Tottenham	13-36	(8-15)
Wimbledon	13-41	(8-20)

Performance level at even money or odds against

FIRST DIVISION

Barnsley	13-40	(8-17)
Birmingham	9-42	(6-19)
Bristol City	11-40	(7-17)
Charlton	10-32	(4-9)
Derby	12-28	(5-6)
Grimsby	15-39	(8-16)
Leicester	12-28	(4-6)
Luton	9-41	(5-18)
Millwall	9-29	(5-7)
Notts County	10-42	(8-19)
Oxford	12-41	(6-18)
Peterborough	12-36	(3-13)
Portsmouth	12-29	(5-6)
Southend	11-44	(7-21)
Sunderland	11-38	(7-15)
Tranmere	13-31	(5-8)
Watford	13-44	(7-21)
Wolves	10-32	(5-9)

Performance level at even money or odds against

SECOND DIVISION

Blackpool	9-40	(6-17)
Bournemouth	9-37	(4-14)
Bradford	12-31	(5-8)
Brighton	11-30	(4-7)
Burnley	8-33	(4-10)
Exeter	8-39	(2-16)
Fulham	10-36	(4-14)
Hartlepool	11-38	(5-15)
Huddersfield	15-42	(8-19)
Hull	8-36	(4-13)
Leyton Orient	11-30	(6-7)
Plymouth	8-34	(3-11)
Port Vale	14-27	(5-8)
Reading	12-37	(8-14)
Rotherham	11-30	(3-7)
Stockport	13-30	(5-7)
Swansea	9-29	(1-6)

Performance level at even money or odds against

THIRD DIVISION

Bury	13-30	(5-9)
Carlisle	9-39	(5-18)
Chesterfield	11-33	(7-12)
Colchester	10-31	(5-11)
Crewe	10-25	(2-4)
Darlington	11-38	(4-17)
Doncaster	10-37	(5-16)
Gillingham	8-40	(8-19)
Hereford	10-41	(7-20)
Lincoln	12-28	(4-7)
Northampton	11-38	(6-17)
Rochdale	13-33	(7-12)
Scarborough	12-31	(4-10)
Scunthorpe	10-33	(4-12)
Shrewsbury	12-29	(6-8)
Torquay	11-39	(5-18)
Walsall	14-26	(3-5)

Performance level at even money or odds against

SCOTTISH PREMIER DIVISION

Aberdeen	10-19	(2-4)
Celtic	10-20	(2-4)
Dundee	8-40	(4-18)
Dundee United	11-30	(0-8)
Hearts	6-29	(3-7)
Hibernian	8-34	(4-12)
Motherwell	10-40	(6-18)
Partick	12-40	(5-18)
Rangers	4-9	(0-1)
St. Johnstone	6-37	(4-15)

Performance level at even money or odds against

SCOTTISH FIRST DIVISION

Ayr	10-35	(6-15)
Clydebank	10-34	(5-13)
Dumbarton	14-40	(9-18)
Dunfermline	13-25	(3-6)
Hamilton	8-28	(2-9)
Morton	8-31	(2-11)
Stirling	10-42	(6-20)
St. Mirren	11-27	(4-9)

Performance level at even money or odds against

SCOTTISH SECOND DIVISION

Albion	6-39	(4-19)
Alloa	9-25	(1-5)
Arbroath	13-30	(4-13)
Berwick	13-32	(5-12)
East Fife	11-30	(3-12)
East Stirling	8-37	(4-18)
Forfar	7-20	(0-2)
Montrose	7-30	(2-11)
Queen of the South	11-35	(4-16)
Queen's Park	8-38	(6-18)
Stenhousemuir	12-32	(6-13)
Stranraer	12-24	(3-6)

Team by team

On the following pages you will find the detailed analysis of all teams in England and Scotland who are competing in the same division as last year.

How to read the sections for each team:

Price performance   A detailed look at the way results went for each team when they were priced up by the bookmakers.

Results when odds on   Number of times a team won a match compared to the number of occasions they started odds on.

Correct score   Repetitive results are outlined that would have given you a profit to level stakes betting:-

First goalscorer   Players are listed who would have given you a good run for your money (and sometimes a profit) in this sector of the betting market.

Teams won against twice   i.e. the teams that they did 'the double' over last year. (Teams in brackets are now in different division)

Teams they lost to twice   As above, only they lost both matches played.

Half-time comparisons   The 'double-result' section of the betting market is very popular nowadays, and these figures will show when teams were winning, drawing or losing at half-time on a regular basis.

Significant numbers   This will show if and when teams have the habit of either scoring or conceding a certain number of goals during the season.

Potentially important matches   Dates for this season's matches are shown which are deemed as vital to the club's cause. The opposition are listed either because of their potential strength and/or they form part of a local 'derby'.

Games they need to win   Matches are listed that are vital to the team's season. Opposition are named that should be beaten if the team in question are to either win the championship, push towards promotion or erase any relegation fears.
They were games that they did not manage to win last season.

Premier Division

ARSENAL

Price Performance

Arsenal's best area in terms of results was the 4/5 & 8/11 sector. They won four of the five matches played when they started at either price.

They won just four matches from fifteen when they started 6/4 or more.

They failed to win a match from seven attempts when they were priced between 11/10 against and 5/6 on.

Results When Odds On

We have touched on this sector in the price performance above. However, Arsenal failed to win at their two shortest prices of the season, at 1/2 when they lost at home to Norwich, and at 8/15 when they drew with Sheffield United at Highbury.

Correct Scores

They lost eleven matches by one goal to nil.

They played in six goal-less draws, and won two home matches by the scoreline of 3-0.

First Goalscorer

You might think that Ian Wright would dominate this section, but he 'only' scored the first goal in a league match on five occasions, which would have lost you money over the season.

A better bet would have been Alan Smith who would have shown a profit given his lack of games.

Teams They Beat Twice

Coventry
Oldham
Manchester City
(Crystal Palace)

Note that teams in brackets will not be competing in the same league this year

ARSENAL

Lost Twice To Last Season
Aston Villa   Tottenham
Blackburn   Wimbledon

Half-time Comparisons
For 'double result' enthusiasts, Arsenal's record at half-time
was:
Leading in   13 matches
Drawing in 18 matches
Losing in   11 matches
They went on to win just four of those 18 drawing opportunities
They were drawing in 7 at home, and never won a game.

Significant Number of Goals
Arsenal failed to score in eleven away matches from their quota
of 21, and never scored more than two goals on their travels.
They conceded a single goal on twenty occasions, ten at home and
ten away.

Important Games This Season
Aug 16 away at Tottenham
Sep 19 away at Man. Utd.
Oct 2 away at Liverpool
Nov 24 away at West Ham
Dec 7 home to Tottenham
Mar 12 home to Man. Utd.
Mar 26 home to Liverpool
Apr 30 home to West Ham

Matches They Need to Win
At home to: Ipswich
               Sheffield United
               Wimbledon

Away to: Wimbledon
               Southampton
               Chelsea

ASTON VILLA

Price Performance

Villa won four out of five games when starting at 11/8, and three out of four when 13/8, so clearly they had a good record in matches that were considered tight by the bookmakers.

They started at 2/1 or better four times without winning.

Results When Odds On

Villa won 4/4 when priced at 4/7 and three out of three when 5/6. They lost when they started at their shortest price in the game against Oldham (2/5)

Correct Scores

Villa featured in five 1-1 draws away from home, and won twice by a 3-2 scoreline on their travels.

First Goalscorer

There was no obvious contender at Villa which might surprise you.

Yorke was always value because of the attention to more senior players, whilst Parker would have made you a profit.

Daley was another option, and was better value than most.

Teams They Beat Twice

Liverpool
(Middlesbrough)
Sheffield United
Arsenal
Wimbledon
(Nottm. Forest)
Sheffield Wednesday

ASTON VILLA

Lost Twice To Last Season

Norwich

Half-time Comparisons

Villa led in 15 matches
Were drawing in 17 matches
And losing in 10 matches
They lost only three matches from those drawing situations.

Significant Number of Goals

Villa kept ten 'clean sheets' in front of their own supporters, and conceded one goal eighteen times throughout the season.

Important Games This Season

Aug 23 home to Man. Utd.
Sep 11 home to Coventry
Nov 6 away at Arsenal
Dec 18 away at Man. Utd.
Mar 5 away at Coventry
Apr 23 home to Arsenal

Matches They Need to Win

At home to: Southampton
                 Chelsea
                 Tottenham
Away to: Everton
                 Coventry
                 Southampton

BLACKBURN ROVERS

Price Performance
They won at their longest price of the season at home, 8/5
(Arsenal). Only drew at the shortest price (5/4) away,at Wimbledon. Won two of the three matches where they were priced
between 2/1 & 13/5. They won four of the five matches where they
were priced 1/1 to 11/8. No other side bettered that record.

Results When Odds On
Blackburn won eight matches from the fifteen when they started
odds on.
That is a percentage of 53.3.

Correct Scores
They won five home matches 1-0 They won two matches 4-1 at
home. They lost 2-3 twice away from home.

First Goalscorers
Mike Newell and Alan Shearer would certainly have made a
profit for you, whilst Ripley and Wilcox made more than just a
contribution.

Teams They Beat Twice
Arsenal
Oldham
Q.P.R.
Sheffield United

BLACKBURN ROVERS

Teams They Lost To Twice
Everton

Half-time Comparisons
Blackburn were only losing in three of their forty two games at
halftime. They were drawing in twenty
four games at the interval, and remained level at the end in most
(eleven) and lost five.
Blackburn lost all three games when they were behind at the
interval.

Significant Number of Goals
Blackburn kept eleven 'clean sheets' in their twenty one home
games. They scored two or more goals nineteen times in both
home and away matches.

Important Games
Aug 25 Manchester City (away)
Sep 12 Liverpool (away)
Dec 18 Manchester City (home)
Dec 26 Manchester United (away)
Mar 5 Liverpool (home)
Apr 2 Manchester United (home)

Matches They Need To Win

At home to:	Tottenham
	Wimbledon
	Coventry
	Southampton
	Everton
Away to:	Ipswich
	Everton

CHELSEA

Price Performance
Chelsea won five of the six games where they were priced between 11/10 and 5/4.

They failed to win a game in eleven attempts when they ranged from 11/8 to 7/4.

On the plus side, they won half the matches (8/16) when they were chalked up from 9/5 to 2/1.

Results When Odds On
They failed to win at their shortest price of 4/6, and won just three games from seven when they ranged between 10/11 and 4/5.

Correct Scores
Chelsea featured in eight 'jackpot' draws which would have yielded a small profit.

First Goalscorers
Harford and Stuart topped the lists for Chelsea without setting the world alight. Stuart would have given us a profit, and Spencer would have given us a decent run for our money.

Teams They Beat Twice
Everton
Coventry

CHELSEA

Lost Twice To Last Season
Norwich
Sheffield United

Half-time Comparisons
Chelsea led in 10 matches
They were drawing 17 matches
And losing in 15 matches
Chelsea only lost two of those 17 matches where they were level
at the interval.

Significant Number of Goals
They conceded two goals or more on fourteen occasions.
They scored one goal eighteen times during the season.

Important Games
Aug 25 home to Q.P.R.
Sep 11 home to Man. Utd.
Nov 20 home to Arsenal
Dec 20 away at Q.P.R.
Mar 5 away at Man. Utd.
Apr 16 away at Arsenal

Matches They Need to Win
At home to: Oldham
                  Sheffield United
                  Southampton
Away to: Oldham
                  Sheffield United
                  Southampton

COVENTRY

Price Performance

Coventry won both matches when they were sent off as 7/2 chances, and also won one of the two games when they were 4/1.

They failed to win in the two matches where they were 9/2 and 11/2.

Their record in matches between the odds of 6/4 and 6/5 was poor. They only won three games from ten in that price band.

Results When Odds On

They started odds on only six times when they won just once (10/11). Having said that their shortest price was only 4/5.

Correct Scores

There was a small profit to be made from a home scoreline of 3-0, whilst they drew four matches 2-2 split equally home and away.

First Goalscorer

Williams and to a lesser extent Quinn would have made money for you over the course of the season.

Gynn can always be relied upon to give you a run for your money.

Teams They Beat Twice

(Middlesbrough)
Tottenham
Oldham
Sheffield Wednesday

COVENTRY

Lost Twice To Last Season
Q.P.R.
Chelsea
Manchester City
Arsenal
Manchester United

Half-time Comparisons
Coventry were leading in 15 matches
They were level in 14 matches
And were losing in 13 matches
They went on to lose 12 of the thirteen matches they were behind in.

Significant Number of Goals
Coventry failed to score in 15 matches which sent them tumbling down the league after a good start to the season.
They managed to score five goals on two occasions though, against Blackburn and Liverpool no less.

Important Games
Aug 14 away at Arsenal
Sep 11 away at Aston Villa
Nov 27 home to Man. Utd.
Dec 4 home to Arsenal
Mar 5 home to Aston Villa
May 7 away at Man. Utd.

Matches They Need to Win
At home to: Q.P.R.
              Ipswich
              Wimbledon
Away to: Sheffield United
              Ipswich
              Southampton

EVERTON

Price Performance

Everton did well when priced at either 9/4 and 13/5. They won no less than five from seven matches in this price band.

They won at 10/3 and 7/2, though they failed to win at either of their biggest prices of 4/1 and 9/2.

Everton only won three matches from eleven starts when they were bracketed between 11/10 and 11/8.

Results When Odds On

It says much about Everton's recent run that they only started odds on in seven games all season. What is more is they only won two of them.

They secured only one point in their two shortest priced games (4/6 & 8/11).

Correct Scores

Everton featured in two 2-2 draws at Goodison, whilst they won 3-0 three times during the course of the season.

They were a team to avoid for pools clients, figuring in only three 1-1 draws and the same number of scoreless matches.

First Goalscorer

Everton only scored the first goal of the match on sixteen occasions, and no one player stood out.

Cottee and Beardsley would have cost you money, though Jackson would have redressed the balance a little.

Teams They Beat Twice

Blackburn
(Nottingham Forest)

EVERTON

Lost Twice To Last Season
Chelsea
Tottenham
Q.P.R.
Sheffield United

Half-time Comparisons
Everton were leading in 11 games
They were drawing in 17 games
and losing in14 games
They went on to lose thirteen of those fourteen losing situations,
though they won the other match at home to Blackburn.

Significant Number of Goals
Everton scored three goals on six occasions winning five of the
games.
They conceded two or more goals on seventeen occasions.
Everton failed to score at home seven times which is well above
average.

Important Games
Sep 18 home to Liverpool
Oct 23 home to Man. Utd.
Dec 28 away at Blackburn
Jan 22 away at Man. Utd.
Mar 12 away at Liverpool
Apr 4 home to Blackburn

Matches They Need to Win
At home: Wimbledon
                     Chelsea
                     Sheffield United
Away at: Oldham
                     Sheffield United
                     Ipswich

IPSWICH

Price Performance

Ipswich won at their only attempt when they were priced at 100/30.

However, this was their only victory in 11 efforts in a price band between 13/5 and 9/2 (their largest price all season)

Another poor performance came when they ranged between 6/4 and 15/8. They won four matches from twelve games in this band.

Results When Odds On

Ipswich managed just one victory (home to Wimbledon) from five efforts when odds on.

They started as warm favourites at 8/13 against Oldham and Middlesbrough and lost both matches. 8/13 was the shortest price they ever were.

Correct Scores

They won four home matches by two goals to one, and also shared four goals at home on two occasions.

They won 3-1 twice at Portman Road, and drew 2-2 twice away from home.

First Goalscorer

Kiwomba and Johnson received their deserved acclaim, and both would have secured a profit on the season.

Teams They Beat Twice

Wimbledon
Norwich
(Nottingham Forest)

IPSWICH

Lost Twice To Last Season
Oldham

Half-time Comparisons
Ipswich were leading in 11 games.
They were drawing in 19 games
And losing in 12 games
They won only five of the matches in which they led, and lost nine of the twelve when they were behind.
This obviously contributed to their decline in the latter half of the season, after a very impressive beginning.

Significant Number of Goals
Ipswich only scored more than one goal fifteen times in their forty two games.
Only four sides failed to score at Ipswich during the season. They were Southampton, Sheffield United, Everton and Coventry.
Ipswich kept nearly twice as many clean sheets away from home as they did at Portman Road.
The defence kept the opposition out seven times away from home.

Important Games This Season
Aug 25 away at Norwich
Sep 11 away at Arsenal
Nov 24 away at Man. Utd.
Dec 18 home to Norwich
Mar 5 home to Arsenal
Apr 30 home to Man. Utd.

Matches They Need to Win

At home:	Southampton
	Oldham
	Chelsea
Away at:	Oldham
	Sheffield United
	Southampton

LEEDS UNITED

Price Performance

The bookmakers took few chances with Leeds on their travels, despite the well documented away form of the Yorkshire outfit. The largest price on offer was just 100/30, which was surprising as they did not win any matches in twelve attempts when priced at 9/5 or more.

They did win three matches from five when they were priced at either 11/10 or 5/4.

Results When Odds On

They won eight from fourteen when well fancied but won just two from five when shading odds on at either 10/11 or 4/5.

Correct Scores

Leeds won twice at both 3-0 and 3-1 at home and lost 0-4 at Manchester City and Tottenham.

On the draw front, they shared four goals twice at home, and drew 3-3 at Coventry.

First Goalscorer

Chapman was a disappointment, though McAllister would have shown a profit.

The other players were all losers as far as we can make out.

Teams They Beat Twice

None

LEEDS UNITED

Lost Twice To Last Season
None

Half-time Comparisons
Leeds led in only 8 matches.
Drawing in 18 matches
And losing in 16 matches
Leeds won only five games from the eighteen they were level in at the interval.

Significant Number of Goals
Leeds kept ten clean sheets at home, but just one away (at Arsenal).
They scored 25 goals in just seven games on one hand, but failed to score nine times away from Elland Road.

Important Games This Season
Sep 18 home to Sheff. Utd.
Oct 30 away to Sheff. Wed.
Jan 1 away at Man. Utd.
Feb 12 home to Sheff. Wed.
Mar 12 away at Sheff. Utd.
Apr 9 home to Man. Utd.

Matches They Need to Win

At home:	Coventry
	Chelsea
	Q.P.R.
Away at:	Sheffield United
	Q. P. R.
	Everton

LIVERPOOL

Price Performance

Liverpool won when at their biggest price of the season (3/1 at Arsenal).

On the other hand, they failed to win in nine attempts when they ranged from 8/5 to 13/5.

They won two from five when priced at either 11/10 or 6/5, and failed to win any of the games where they started at either 5/4 or 11/8 which they did on four occasions.

Results When Odds On

Liverpool came good in this sector, though they did only draw at their season's shortest price of 4/7.

The most impressive price band came in the 4/5 to 8/13 sector. They won eight of the nine matches they contested at these prices.

Correct Scores

They won by four goals to one twice at home, and drew 2-2 three times on their travels.

First Goalscorer

They scored the first goal of the match twenty one times, but unfortunately there were too many players contributing to make much profit.

Hutchison was probably your best bet, and Rosenthal when he was given the opportunity.

Teams They Beat Twice

Q.P.R
(Middlesbrough)

LIVERPOOL

Lost Twice To Last Season
Wimbledon
Aston Villa

Half-time Comparisons
Liverpool led in just 10 matches
They were drawing in 22 matches
And losing in 10 matches
They won 10 of the games they were level in at half-time.
Liverpool rescued just two points from the ten matches where they were behind.

Significant Number Of Goals
Three of London's teams were the only sides who failed to score against Liverpool on their travels.
Chelsea, Arsenal and Q.P.R. all failed,whereas the other eighteen teams managed to score a total of 37 when entertaining Liverpool.
Liverpool failed to score more than one goal twenty six times in their forty two matches.

Important Games This Season
Sep 18 away at Everton
Oct 2 home to Arsenal
Jan 3 home to Man. Utd.
Mar 12 home to Everton
Mar 26 away at Arsenal
Mar 30 away at Man. Utd.

Matches They Need to Win

At home:	Southampton
	Wimbledon
	Manchester City
Away at:	Oldham
	Ipswich
	Sheffield United
	Tottenham
	Coventry

MANCHESTER CITY

Price Performance

Manchester City won four of the six games they played when they were priced at 6/4.

They won two of the three matches when they were either 5/2 or 11/4.

They lost in all three games where they started at their largest odds. They failed at 3/1, 100/30 and 5/1.

They won both games where they went off at 7/4.

Results When Odds On

They started at 5/6 on six occasions and won only two against Southampton and Coventry.

Their shortest price was 4/6 where they recorded one win from two starts.

It was the same story when they started at 4/5.

Correct Scores

A 3-3 home draw early in the season would have paid for the year's entertainment, whilst five jackpot draws at Maine Road would have secured a small profit.

They lost 1-3 three times away from home.

First Goalscorer

David White (alongside Mike Newell) was the toast of the division in this department.

Sheron and Flitcroft were also worth following.

Teams They Beat Twice

Coventry
Southampton

MANCHESTER CITY

Lost Twice To Last Season
(Middlesbrough)
Tottenham
Arsenal

Half-time Comparisons
Man. City were leading in 16 matches
They were drawing in 12 matches
And losing in 14 matches.
They did well to win three and draw two of those 14 deficits, but managed to win only three times from the twelve drawing situations.

Significant Number of Goals
Manchester City scored one goal nineteen times, and conceded a goal on eighteen occasions.
Little wonder then that they featured in eight jackpot draws.
They failed to score as many times at home as they did away (5).

Important Games This Season
Aug 25 home to Blackburn
Oct 23 home to Liverpool
Nov 7 home to Man. Utd.
Dec 18 away at Blackburn
Jan 22 away at Liverpool
Apr 23 away at Man. Utd.

Matches They Need to Win
At home: Chelsea
               Tottenham
               Everton
Away at: Ipswich
               Q.P.R.
               Norwich

MANCHESTER UNITED

Price Performance

Manchester United won three from six when starting at 11/8, and were victorious in two matches from the four that they were priced up at 6/4.

They won at their biggest price of the season which was 9/4 at Highbury.

Results When Odds On

Manchester United started odds on in nineteen of their twenty one home matches, and were the only team in the league to start an away game at odds on.

They won all eight matches where they started at their shortest prices which ranged from 4/7 to 2/5.

They were chalked up at 4/6 three times and won the lot, but failed to win at either 8/11 or 8/13 on five occasions.

They won two of the three away games at 10/11 and 4/5, but lost the shortest priced match (8/11) at Oldham.

Correct Scores

Manchester United had three home victories by the score of 3-0, and won twice away fron home 3-1. They fought their way back from 3-0 down at Hillsborough to grab a draw which would have paid for the season to a level stake.

First Goalscorer

Mark Hughes grabbed the initiative and was a winner for his followers, as was Paul Ince and Ryan Giggs.

Teams They Beat Twice

Southampton
(Nottingham Forest)
Norwich
Coventry
(Crystal Palace)

MANCHESTER UNITED

Lost Twice To Last Season
None

Half-time Comparisons
United were leading in 16 matches
They were drawing in 18 matches
and losing in just 8 matches
They won fourteen of those games where they were in front, dropping just four points from a potential forty eight.
They also won nine of the eighteen where they were level, and lost just one at home to Wimbledon.

Significant Number of Goals
They scored the first goal of the match in over half of their games (22), and kept eighteen clean sheets.
They only conceded more than one goal five times, and two of those were in their opening pair of games!

Important Games This Season
Aug 23 away at Aston Villa
Sep 19 home to Arsenal
Nov 7 away at Manchester City
Dec 18 home to Aston Villa
Mar 12 away at Arsenal
Apr 23 home to Manchester City

Matches They Need to Win
At home: Everton
                Ipswich
                Wimbledon
Away at: Sheffield United
                Ipswich
                Oldham

NORWICH

Price Performance

Norwich started surprising people in the very first game of the season at Highbury. Priced at 6/1 (easily the biggest price of the season), they were two goals down at Arsenal with only 23 minutes to play. The fact that they won 4-2 is now history.

They also won at their next largest price (3/1) at Aston Villa.

They won all three games when priced at 6/5, and two from three when 7/4 chances.

Results When Odds On

Norwich started at odds on thirteen times which could not have been predicted before the season started.

They won eight of those matches, including the three matches where they started as 'bankers', priced at 4/7 8/13 and 4/6.

Correct Scores

They won five home matches by two goals to one, and another couple 4-2.

They won three away matches by three goals to two at Chelsea, Oldham and Aston Villa.

First Goalscorer

Mark Robins was rewarding his followers before his injury, and could have given Messers White and Newell a run for their money had he stayed sound.

Fox, Crook, Sutton and Phillips all gave their supporters value for money.

Teams They Beat Twice

Chelsea	(Nottingham Forest)
Sheffield United	Oldham
(Crystal Palace)	Aston Villa

NORWICH

Lost Twice To Last Season
Ipswich   Manchester United

Half-time Comparisons
Norwich were leading in 9 matches
They were drawing in 21 matches
And losing in 12 matches
Norwich turned 11 of those drawing situations into wins, and salvaged three wins from the matches where they were adrift at the interval.

Significant Number of Goals
Norwich always gave their opponents a chance to beat them as they leaked goals consistantly.
Only four sides failed to score against them away from Carrow Road, they were Leeds, Everton, Nottingham Forest and Sheffield United.
However, they could certainly score them as well, and they chalked up nineteen goals in just six away games.

Important Games This Season
Aug 15 home to Man. Utd.
Aug 25 home to Ipswich
Dec 4 away at Man. Utd.
Dec 18 away at Ipswich
Dec 28 home to Aston Villa
Apr 4 away to Aston Villa

Matches They Need to Win
At home: Everton
                  Ipswich
                  Coventry
Away at: Coventry
                  Southampton
                  Wimbledon

OLDHAM

Price Performance

Oldham won at the two biggest prices that were chalked against their name.

They started at 11/2 at Villa and 9/2 at Ipswich and won them both.

They won five games from seven when priced at either 6/5 or 5/4, but fared poorly in the band between 7/4 and 2/1. Here they played in six games and failed to win any of them.

Results When Odds On

They only started odds on in two matches and even then only because of circumstance

They lost 0-1 to Coventry at odds of 5/6 and then beat Southampton 4-3 when 2/5 favourites. Oldham had something to play for and The Saints didn't. Instead of being 2/5, Oldham would have been around even money at any other stage of the season.

Correct Scores

They drew four matches 2-2 during the season, and shared six goals at Maine Road.

Oldham were beaten 2-0 five times on their travels, and lost 2-3 on one occasion both home and away.

First Goalscorer

Despite scoring plenty of goals, Oldham lacked a consistent man to net the all important first goal.

Henry was the only man you would have wanted to have been on.

Teams They Beat Twice

Ipswich
(Middlesbrough)

OLDHAM

Lost Twice To Last Season

Coventry   Norwich
Blackburn   Arsenal

Half-time Comparisons

Oldham were leading in 19 matches
They were drawing in 11 matches
And losing in 12 matches
Oldham once again produce the amazing facts.
They were the only premier side not to have been losing in their home matches at half-time.
For reasons that only Joe Royle probably knows, Oldham were behind in 12 of their matches away from home. They only rescued one point from those matches.
They also failed to win a single game from eleven half-time drawing situations.

Significant Number of Goals

Oldham's home record was amazing!
They conceded just six goals in all 21 home matches in the first half. In the second half they let in 24.
Fortunately, they scored 43 themselves at Boundary Park, but just twenty away from home.

Important Games This Season

Aug 21 away at Blackburn
Oct 2 away at Man. City
Dec 11 home to Blackburn
Dec 28 home to Man. Utd.
Mar 26 home to Man. City
Apr 4 away at Man. Utd.

Matches They Needed to Win

At home: Coventry   Manchester City
                Sheffield United
Away at: Southampton   Sheffield United
                Coventry

63

Q.P.R.

Price Performance

Q.P.R. only won once in twelve attempts when starting at 2/1 or more. On that occasion they put five goals past Everton at Goodison when chalked up at 12/5.

They had a good record when priced at 6/4 with three wins from four starts.

Q.P.R. won all four games when priced at either 11/10 or 6/5.

Results When Odds On

Considering Q.P.R. finished a very creditable fifth in the league, they were generously priced up throughout the season.

They only started odds on seven times winning in three of them.

They failed at 5/6 on both occasions, but won two out of three when starting at their shortest price of 8/11.

Correct Scores

Q.P.R. lost 0-1 five times away from home, whilst they shared six goals at Loftus Road with Middlesbrough.

Their other home scorelines included 3-1 three times and 3-2 twice.

All of these scores would have produced a profit to level stake betting throughout the season.

First Goalscorer

Les Ferdinand had a great season and would have rewarded his fans, whilst Allen and Impey followers were on the 'right side'.

Teams They Beat Twice

Southampton
Sheffield United
Coventry
Everton

Q.P.R.

Lost Twice To Last Year
Liverpool   Blackburn

Half-time Comparisons
Q.P.R. were leading in 14 matches
They were drawing in 14 matches
And losing in 14 matches
They held on to win 11 times when in front, but only won twice from the 14 drawing situations.
To their credit Q.P.R. also rescued sixteen points from those games where they were behind.

Significant Number of Goals
Only three teams failed to score against Q.P.R. at Loftus Road. They were Arsenal, Ipswich and Coventry. Rangers still managed to win eleven home games though, scoring 41 goals in the process.
They scored 30 goals in just nine of those thus they scored 11 times in the twelve other matches.

Important Games This Season
Aug 25 away at Chelsea
Oct 30 away at Man. Utd.
Dec 20 home to Chelsea
Jan 3 away at Arsenal
Feb 12 home to Man. Utd.
Mar 30 home to Arsenal

Matches They Need to Win
At home: Ipswich
                   Manchester City
                   Wimbledon
Away at: Chelsea
                   Ipswich
                   Oldham

SHEFFIELD UNITED

Price Performance

Sheffield United won just one match (away to Chelsea) when they were priced at 11/4 or more. They played eleven such games and were 3/1 when winning at Stamford Bridge.

They won five matches from nine when they were bracketed between 11/8 and 13/8.

Results When Odds On

Sheffield only started at odds on five times, but managed to win three of them. The teams they failed to beat were Wimbledon (8/11) and Crystal Palace (10/11).

They beat Chelsea when 8/11 which, along with the Wimbledon game, was their shortest price of the season.

Correct Scores

They lost 0-2 five times on their travels, while they also lost 2-3 (twice) and 1-3 (twice) away from Brammel Lane.

Apart from the 6-0 win over Tottenham, there were no significant home scorelines to report.

First Goalscorers

Sheffield United will be remembered for scoring the first goal in the Premier Division (Deane), rather than the number of times their players found the net.

You would not have lost too much money backing Deane through the season, though Littlejohn and Carr would have been the players to invest in.

Teams They Beat Twice

Everton
Chelsea

SHEFFIELD UNITED

Lost Twice to Last Year

Aston Villa   Q.P.R.
Norwich   (Crystal Palace)
Blackburn

Half-time Comparisons

Sheffield were leading in 14 matches
They were drawing in 12 matches
And losing in 16 matches
Most of Sheffield's problems came from those games that they were level in at half-time. They only managed to convert two of the twelve into victories, though they did secure five draws.
They salvaged six points from a possible forty eight when they were behind, and hung on to win eleven of those 14 leading situations.

Significant Number of Goals

Only Ipswich, Everton and Nottingham Forest failed to score against United when entertaining the Yorkshire club.
Two goals will usually win a Premier match and Sheffield conceded two or more too often.
They conceded two on twelve occasions (eight away from home), and two or more seventeen times.

Important Games This Season

Aug 18 away at Man. Utd.
Sep 18 away at Leeds
Oct 23 home to Sheff. Wed.
Dec 7 home to Man. Utd.
Jan 22 away to Sheff. Wed.
Mar 12 home to Leeds

Matches They Need to Win

At home:	Coventry	Q.P.R.
	Manchester City	
Away at:	Wimbledon	Southampton
	Oldham	

SHEFFIELD WEDNESDAY

Price Performance
Wednesday failed to win in their nine longest priced matches. You had to work down to 15/8 before you came across two victories (from two) against Southampton and Tottenham (both away).

They only won twice from six efforts when priced at 6/4, though they won on the solitary occasions that they started at evens, 5/4 and 11/8.

Results When Odds On
Sheffield generally disappointed when odds on. They only won five times from the twelve games they played, though they did win at their shortest price of 4/7 against Crystal Palace.

They only won two from five when 4/5 chances, and lost both games (Manchester City and Middlesbrough) when starting at 5/6.

Correct Scores
Wednesday were the jackpot draw kings of the Premier Division. They drew 1-1 eleven times (six of them away), and drew 3-3 at home to both Manchester United and Chelsea.

First Goalscorers
Whilst Paul Warhurst rightly got his share of the limelight, Mark Bright was knocking in the first goal on many occasions and would have paid his way.

Hirst would have given you a run for your money, but really Bright was the man to be on in this department.

Teams They Beat Twice
(Nottingham Forest)
Tottenham
Southampton

SHEFFIELD WEDNESDAY

Lost Twice To Last Year

Coventry   Aston Villa

Half-time Comparisons

Wednesday were leading in 16 matches.

They were drawing in 13 matches

And losing in 13 matches

They only won three of the games where they were level, which probably explains why they finished down in seventh place. They undoubtedly have potential to finish much higher in the league than that.

Wednesday let four of their winning situations turn into draws which was also disappointing.

However, they did salvage five draws from the 13 games they trailed in at half-time.

Significant Number of Goals

Only Tottenham, Chelsea and Ipswich failed to score against Wednesday on their travels, though they still managed to win six games.

On the plus front, Wednesday only failed to score on two occasions in front of their fans, and they managed to score two goals in ten games.

They conceded a single goal 21 times.

Important Games This Season

Oct 2 home to Man. Utd.

Oct 23 away at Sheff. Utd.

Oct 30 home to Leeds

Jan 22 home to Sheff. Utd.

Feb 12 away at Leeds

Mar 26 away at Man. Utd.

Matches They Need to Win

At home:	Coventry	Away at:	Norwich
	Sheffield United		Coventry
	Wimbledon		Oldham

SOUTHAMPTON

Price Performance

Southampton started thirteen games at 11/4 or more, and failed to win any of them.

Their biggest price all season was when they were 5/1 to win at Old Trafford. They took the lead after 77 minutes, but couldn't hold on eventually losing to the odd goal in three.

They won both times they were priced at 2/1 (at home to Villa and away at Wimbledon), and they also won all three times when they were 5/4 chances.

Results When Odds On

Southampton only started as odds on favourites four times, and they won two of them against Sheffield United and Ipswich. In the other games, they drew with Coventry and lost to Forest, starting at 10/11 in both matches.

Their shortest price came in the match with Sheffield United, where they scraped home 3-2 at 5/6.

Correct Scores

Southampton shared four goals in two home matches (against Coventry and Wimbledon),

They lost 3-4 away from home on two occasions (at Arsenal and Oldham), and beat Ipswich 4-3 at The Dell.

First Goalscorer

Predictably, Matt Le Tissier was in charge in this department, though Dowie, Maddison and Banger would have made you more profit over the course of the season.

Teams They Beat Twice

(Crystal Palace)

SOUTHAMPTON

Lost Twice To Last Season

Manchester United   Q.P.R.
Sheffield Wednesday   Manchester City

Half-time Comparisons

Southampton were leading in 12 matches
They were drawing in 18 matches
And losing in 12 matches
The Saints did well to only lose four of the drawing situations at
the interval, though they would have liked to have won more
than six games from the twelve in which they led.
They only won four points from a possible thirty six when they
were behind at half-time.

Significant Number of Goals

Southampton let in their fair share of goals, and were the only
team that Arsenal scored more than three goals against. Even
then, they were a goal up in four minutes, though they had
conceded three by the interval.
Only Ipswich and Blackburn failed to score against Southampton when they left the south coast, and both of those games were
0-0 draws.
They conceded forty goals away from home, and twenty five of
those came in the second half.

Important Games This Year

Aug 28 home to Man. Utd.
Sep 25 away at Arsenal
Oct 30 away at Liverpool
Feb 12 home to Liverpool
Feb 19 away at Man. Utd.
Mar 19 home to Arsenal

Matches They Need to Win

At home: Q.P.R.   Away at: Sheffield United
             Coventry   Coventry
             Manchester City   Chelsea

TOTTENHAM

Price Performance

Tottenham won all four games where they started at even money, and good priced victories came at Blackburn (100/30) and Manchester City (13/5)

They started four games in the price band between 11/10 and 5/4 and failed to win any and lost three.

Their most common price was 13/8 which they started at seven times, winning three. They won both their matches when 7/4 chances at Everton and Arsenal.

Results When Odds On

Such was their inconsistency, that Tottenham only started at odds on in six games, of which they won three.

They lost at their shortest price which was 8/11 against Coventry in their first home game of the season.

Correct Scores

I could certainly think of doing better things with my money than to invest in Tottenham's correct score games.

Losing 0-6 at Sheffield United, 0-5 at Leeds and 2-6 at Liverpool should prove my point.

First Goalscorers

Teddy Sheringham stood head and shoulders above the other players in terms of goals.

Whilst you were making a profit on the ex-Forest striker though, you would have suffered major losses backing any of the others at White Hart Lane.

Teams They Beat Twice

Everton
Manchester City
Arsenal

TOTTENHAM

Lost Twice To Last Season

Coventry   Sheffield Wednesday

Half-time Comparisons

Tottenham were leading in 12 matches
They were drawing in 14 matches
And losing in 16 matches
Tottenham finished eighth in the league, but would have figured better but for their inability to turn draws at the interval into victories. They won just four after being level, though they improved sufficiently in the second half to win three and draw three from their sixteen first half deficits.

Significant Number of Goals

Spurs fans will tell you that the four goals they scored against Arsenal were the significant goals of the season. These enabled Tottenham to do 'the double' over their arch rivals despite The Gunners cup exploits.
Tottenham conceded 25 goals in just five matches away from home, hence the new manager has a little work to do before the new season.
Spurs scored over two thirds of their home goals in the second half. They also failed to score fourteen times in the opening half of their away matches.

Important Games This Season

Aug 16 home to Arsenal
Oct 16 away at Man. Utd.
Dec 7 away at Arsenal
Dec 28 away at West Ham
Jan 15 home to Man. Utd.
Apr 4 home to West Ham

Matches They Need to Win

At home: Coventry   Away at: Southampton
            Chelsea   Wimbledon
            Ipswich   Oldham

WIMBLEDON

Price Performance

Wimbledon were the exception to the rule as usual. Winning matches they shouldn't and generally proving to be as popular as John Major.

Never a team to leave out, they proved once again that on their day they are a match for any team in the country.

Their away performances were incredible.

They won at Manchester United (9/2), Liverpool (100/30) and Arsenal (4/1) amongst others.

How then, can they get walloped at Oldham (7/4), Crystal Palace (7/4) and Middlesbrough (13/5)?

Results When Odds On

Wimbledon (always a result for the layer) are nearly always a better price than their form respects.

They only started one match at odds on which they won beating Sheffield United when 10/11.

Correct Scores

They beat Arsenal at home and Liverpool away by the same scoreline, which was 3-2.

Wimbledon shared four goals twice on their travels, and also featured in four jackpot draws away from home.

Teams They Beat Twice

Arsenal
Liverpool

WIMBLEDON

Lost Twice To Last Year
Ipswich   Aston Villa

Half-time Comparisons
Wimbledon were leading in 11 matches
they were drawing in 21 matches
and losing in 10 matches
Wimbledon's ability not to win from drawing situations let them
down badly.
They won only five times when level, though they hung on to a
lead well enough. They dropped just four points from a possible
thirty three when in front at the turn.
Wimbledon lost eight of the games in which they trailed, and
managed just two draws.

Significant Number of Goals
They conceded two goals fourteen times during the season which
is too many.
Wimbledon lost ten matches by a single goal, six of them at home.
Liverpool obviously view Wimbledon as some kind of bogey
team, and it will give their manager a nightmare or three if he
finds out that Liverpool conceded the same number of goals last
season, as Wimbledon namely fifty five.

Important Games This Season
Aug 17 home to Chelsea
Nov 20 away at Man. Utd.
Dec 8 away at Chelsea
Jan 1 home to Arsenal
Apr 9 away at Arsenal
Apr 16 home to Man. Utd.

Matches They Need to Win
At home: Ipswich   Away at: Norwich
                  Everton   Manchester City
                  Southampton   Oldham

First Division

BARNSLEY

Price Performance

Barnsley won two matches from five when priced at 13/5, and managed two victories from nine games at bigger prices. The games they won were at Notts County (100/30) and at Millwall (4/1).

The price band that let them down ranged between 6/5 and 12/5. Barnsley won just five games from twenty one matches in this sector of their odds.

Results When Odds On

Barnsley had a good record in the handful of games where they started at odds on.

They won four of their six matches, including the games where they started at their shortest prices of 4/6 (Bristol Rovers) and 4/5 (Bristol City).

They lost the two matches where they were 5/6, but won both at 10/11.

Correct Scores

Barnsley lost 0-3 in three away matches, and won 3-1 three times in all.

A single goal decided eight of their matches, with an even split between victory and defeat.

First Goalscorers

Biggins ruled the roost for Barnsley, and would have rewarded his followers handsomely.

Rammell and O'Connell also featured well in this department.

Teams They Beat Twice

(Cambridge)
(Bristol Rovers)

BARNSLEY

Lost Twice To Last Season

Wolves   Leicester
Grimsby

Half-time Comparisons

Barnsley were leading in 14 matches
They were drawing in 15 matches
And losing in 17 matches
The score at half-time generally dictated the match in Barnsley's case.
They won 13 of the 14 games they led in, and lost 14 of the 17 where they were behind.
Barnsley need to improve when they go in all square at the break. They won just three games from 15 when they were level, though they hung on for a draw seven times.
Barnsley led in eight games at home by half-time and won them all.

Significant Number of Goals

Barnsley lost seven away games by a single goal and a further six by two goals or more.
At home, they won five matches by two goals or more.
Barnsley's goals were very evenly split between the two forty five minute periods. They scored 29 goals in the first half of their matches, and 27 in the second half.

Important Games This Season

Sep 11 home to Nottm. Forest
Sep 25 home to Leicester
Dec 27 home to Derby
Mar 16 away at Nottm Forest
Mar 19 away at Leicester
Apr 2 away at Derby

Matches They Need to Win

At home: Peterborough   Away at: Sunderland
               Watford   Southend
               Oxford   Bristol City

BIRMINGHAM

Price Performance

Birmingham failed to win any of their fourteen matches where they started at their biggest prices (between 5/2 and 8/1).

They won three times from five when priced at 6/4.

They failed to win in five starts in the price band between 13/8 and 15/8, actually losing four of them.

Their biggest priced victory was at 9/4 when they beat Sunderland at Roker Park by two goals to one.

Results When Odds On

Perhaps the supporters at Birmingham can blame the bookmakers for their very average season.

When the layers fancied Brum to win Birmingham obliged. They won all four games where they started at odds on. The teams they beat were Charlton (1/2) Grimsby (4/6), Southend (4/6) and Bristol Rovers (8/11).

Correct Scores

Birmingham featured in four goal-less draws away from home. They lost three away games by one goal in three, and also lost 2-3 twice at home.

First Goalscorers

Peshilsolido and Saville just about paid their way through scoring the first goal of the game was not Birmingham's strong point. They scored first just 19 times from 46 matches.

Teams They Beat Twice

Sunderland

BIRMINGHAM

Lost Twice To Last Season

Wolves	Leicester
Portsmouth	Bristol City
(West Ham)	

Half-time Comparisons

Birmingham were leading in 12 matches
They were drawing in 17 matches
And losing in 17 matches
They won seven of the games where they were in front at the interval, and lost 13 of the 17 where they were behind.
They lost four and won six of the games where they level at the break.

Significant Number of Goals

Birmingham lost twelve games by two goals or more which tells the tale of a sorry season. In a fiercely competitive league they will have to improve or face the ultimate drop, which would disappoint so many loyal supporters.
Birmingham had an exact split with goals tally both home and away. They scored 15 in each half at home during the season, and ten either side of the interval in their away games.

Important Games This Season

Aug 21 home to Wolves
Sep 11 away to Leicester
Dec 28 home to West Brom.
Feb 22 away at Wolves
Mar 15 home to Leicester
Apr 4 away at West Brom.

Matches They Need to Win

At home:		Away at:	
	Wolves		Southend
	Millwall		Notts County
	Bristol City		Watford

BRISTOL CITY

Price Performance

City won their match when priced at 11/2 (away at Portsmouth), but understandably failed to win both times they started at 6/1. Their best performances came when they started at warm favourites in the 11/10 and 6/5 price bands. They won their only game at 11/10, and won two from three at 6/5, losing to Peterborough at home.

Other victories included a win at Derby early on in the season when they were 3/1, and they also won on the solitary occasion they started at 11/5 which was away at Luton.

Results When Odds On

City had a fifty per cent record in the games where they started odds on.

They beat Barnsley (10/11), Notts County (4/5) and Birmingham (10/11).

They failed to win against Luton, Southend and Cambridge.

They won two of the three games when starting at 10/11.

Correct Scores

City featured in five 0-0 draws away from home, and four in front of their own fans.

They won by the odd goal of three five times at home, and lost 1-2 five times on their travels.

First Goalscorer

Cole and Morgan faired best, but scoring first in just fifteen matches does not give a team many winning opportunities.

Teams They Beat Twice

Birmingham

BRISTOL CITY

Lost Twice To Last Season

(West Ham)   Tranmere
(Newcastle)   Millwall

Half-time Comparisons

Bristol City were leading in 6 matches
They were drawing in 24 matches
And losing in 16 matches

The half time story says it all really. City's failure to take hold of a match early on went against them, and certainly made life difficult for their supporters.

They won five of their six matches when in front which is commendable, but unfortunately they lost 14 of the 16 games they trailed in. To their credit they lost only three games from the 24 drawing situations, though no less than 14 of these games remained level at full time.

Significant Number of Goals

City failed to score in ten matches away from home, and only scored one goal in ten more. It is no wonder that they won just four games on their travels.

Bristol conceded 25 goals at home, though only eight of those came in the second half of their matches.

Important Games This Season

Aug 28 away at Derby
Sep 25 away at Portsmouth
Dec 28 home to Nottm. Forest
Mar 5 home to Derby
Mar 19 home to Portsmouth
Apr 4 away at Nottm. Forest

Matches They Need to Win

At home: Southend   Away at: Barnsley
            Peterborough   Sunderland
            Millwall   Oxford

CHARLTON

Price Performance

Charlton won the three games where they were priced at either 6/5 or 11/8.

They failed to win in six starts when priced at 100/30 or more, their biggest winning price being at 11/4 when they won at Oxford.

Charlton won their only game at even money (home to Swindon), and their solitary game at 9/5 away at Cambridge.

Results When Odds On

Considering they finished down in twelfth place, the bookmakers took few chances when pricing up Charlton. They started odds on in 14 matches and won six of them.

They started at 8/13 (shortest price all season) four times and won two of them. They disappointed when 4/5 (two from six) and at 10/11 (no wins from two outings).

Correct Scores

They lost by the only goal of the game six times away from home, and three times in front of their own fans.

There were four matches at home that failed to produce a goal, though they won by three goals to one on two occasions against Grimsby (opening match of the season) and Watford.

First Goalscorer

Pardew was the man to follow in Charlton's away games. He scored the first goal of the game four times, and they were all scored in away fixtures.

Nelson was the only other regular contributor.

Teams They Beat Twice

(Bristol Rovers)

CHARLTON

Lost Twice To Last Season

Millwall   Wolves

Half-time Comparisons

Charlton were leading in nine matches
They were drawing in 24 matches
And losing in 13 matches
Charlton were in front in five games at home at the interval and
won all of them. They won eight of the nine games when in front.
There was fair split between the drawing situations, with
Charlton winning seven and losing eight. Nine matches re-
mained level.
They salvaged six points from the games where they were behind
at the break.

Significant Number of Goals

Charlton lost nine away games by a single goal.
They scored two goals in eleven matches, and actually won eight
of them, and drew the other three.
Of the 28 goals Charlton scored at home, they only netted eight
times in the first period. Another twenty goals came in the
second half, which helped Charlton to win twice as many games
as they lost at home (10-5).

Important Games This Season

Aug 17 away at Portsmouth
Sep 11 home to Millwall
Sep 25 home to Crystal Palace
Dec 11 home to Portsmouth
Mar 16 away at Millwall
Mar 19 away at Crystal Palace

Matches They Need to Win

At home: Luton   Away at: Barnsley
            Sunderland   Notts County
            Wolves   Birmingham

DERBY

Price Performance

Quite simply, the bookmakers never take chances with Derby County of late.

They were the market leaders (or thereabouts) before last season started, and once again they are in pole position in the ante-post books despite fierce opposition.

They flattered only to deceive so many times last year, which was reflected in their price from week to week.

Their biggest price all season was 100/30, though they didn't win a game over 15/8.

They won all three games when sent off at even money, and two from three at 5/4 and three from six at 6/4.

Results When Odds On

They won their only away game at odds on when they beat Bristol Rovers, but it was a much different story in matches at the Baseball Ground.

They won just six matches from seventeen attempts.

They won only four matches between the prices of 8/11 and 4/9 even though they played in twelve matches at those prices.

Derby actually lost home matches at 4/9 (Oxford) and 4/7 (Sunderland), though they won twice from three efforts at 5/6.

Correct Scores

Derby lost 1-2 four times at home, and drew 1-1 four times on their travels.

First Goalscorer

Kitson and Johnson (away) were the men to follow.

Teams They Beat Twice

(Swindon)	Grimsby	(Bristol Rovers)
Notts County	Wolves	

Lost Twice To Last Season

Peterborough	Millwall	Sunderland
Tranmere	Portsmouth	

DERBY

Half-time Comparisons

Derby were leading in 15 matches
They were drawing in 22 matches
And losing in 9 matches
The fact that Derby finished in eighth place was probably due to their drawing situations at half time.

They only turned eight matches into victories from twenty two opportunities. They managed to lose nine of those games and drew the other five.

Derby let the opposition off the hook too often as well. They won just nine games from the fifteen that they led in, having scored the first goal of the game 23 times in the 42 matches that produced goals.

Significant Number of Goals

The bookmakers can only be making Derby favourites through potential rather than form.

They have obviously studied their subject and reacted accordingly.

On the face of last seasons results, Derby are entitled to be up there in the betting, but favouritism is probably flattering them slightly. Sure enough, they did lose 15 games by just one goal and won 13 by two goals or more. We shall see.

Important Games This Year

Aug 18 away at Nottm. Forest
Oct 2 home to West Brom
Oct 16 away at Portsmouth
Dec 11 home to Nottm. Forest
Jan 15 home to Portsmouth
Mar 26 away at West Brom.

Matches They Need to Win

At home: Bristol City   Away at: Southend
             Sunderland   Birmingham
             Luton   Peterborough

GRIMSBY

Price Performance

Grimsby were 7/1 when they brought Newcastle's wonderful start to the season to an abrubt end at St. James' Park.

They won many admirers in the first division last year despite only finishing ninth.

They won two from four at odds of 2/1, and also won at 9/4 (at Watford) and 11/4 (at Barnsley).

Grimsby won both their matches at 11/10, but only one from five attempts at even money. They won one from one at 5/4, 11/8 and 8/5.

Results When Odds On

Grimsby won all four games when priced at either 5/6 or 4/5. They won four from seven attempts all told.

They failed at their three shortest prices of 8/13 (Birmingham), 4/6 (Brentford) and 8/11 (Notts county).

Correct Scores

They lost 1-2 six times on their travels, which contibuted to eleven away games lost by a single goal.

They drew four home games 1-1, and scored the only goal of the game five times in front of their own supporters.

They shared six goals with Notts County at home.

First Goalscorers

Mendonca was the chap to follow as Grimsby scored the first goal of the game on 23 occasions.

Rodger and Dobbin also featured, while Woods paid his way towards the end of the season.

Teams They Beat Twice

Watford
(Bristol Rovers)
Luton
Barnsley

GRIMSBY

Lost Twice To Last Season

Peterborough   Leicester
Derby

Half-time Comparisons

Grimsby were leading in 10 matches
They were drawing in 20 matches
And losing in 16 matches
Grimsby excelled in games which were level at half time. They turned 11 games into victory from such a position, and lost just five.
They lost 13 of the games where they were behind, and won seven of the ten where they led at the interval.

Significant Number of Goals

There was an amazing turn around in Grimsby's matches after the interval.
Grimsby featured in eighteen goal-less first half games, yet only played in one 0-0 draw all season (home to Tranmere).
They scored 33 goals in their home matches, of which 24 came in the second half.

Important Games This Season

Aug 21 away at Nottm. Forest
Nov 2 home to Leicester
Nov 20 away at Derby
Feb 22 home to Nottm. Forest
Apr 16 away at Leicester
Apr 23 home to Derby

Matches They Need to Win

At home: Peterborough   Away at: Sunderland
               Birmingham   Peterborough
               Oxford   Southend

LEICESTER

Price Performance

Leicester's biggest price of the season was just 4/1 which was testament to their good showing throughout the year.

They won three times from five starts when they ranged from even money to 6/5.

Leicester won two from five at 6/4, and two from three at 13/8 (drew away at Oxford).

They won on the only occasion they were sent off at 2/1 (away at Sunderland), and did the same when 11/10 at home to Swindon Town.

Results When Odds On

Leicester started odds on in just one away game. This was when they started at 10/11 at Peterborough where they lost by three goals to nil.

They started odds on seventeen times at home and won ten of them. They failed to win at their shortest price of 2/5, but won five of the six matches where they ranged from 5/6 to 8/11.

They only won one game in three when priced at 4/6 and again at 4/7.

Correct Scores

Leicester lost 0-3 on three occasions on their travels, and also got beaten 0-2 four times away from home.

They won 3-2 four times during the season, with an even split between home and away games.

First Goalscorer

Joachim received much of the attention and would have shown a profit to a level stake.

Walsh, and to a lesser degree Davison were probably better value though.

Teams They Beat Twice

Barnsley	Watford	Birmingham
Sunderland	Grimsby	

LEICESTER

Lost Twice To Last Season
Peterborough   (West Ham)

Half-time Comparisons
Leicester were leading in 16 matches
They were drawing in 19 matches
And losing in 11 matches
Leicester hung on to win in 12 of those 16 games, and lost just the
one to Bristol City (away from home).
They did well to win nine matches from the nineteen drawing
situations, losing only three times.
Leicester rather lost their way when they trailed at half time.
They lost ten of the eleven matches, and lost all eight where they
were behind away from home.

Significant Number of Goals
Leicester scored two or more goals on fourteen occasions at
home, winning thirteen of them. They drew the other game with
Cambridge where they shared four goals.
They lost by two or more goals nine times on their travels, which
is a considerable number for a team who so narrowly missed
promotion.

Important Games This Season
Oct 23 home to Nottingham Forest
Nov 27 home to Wolves
Dec 28 away at Derby
Feb 5 away to Nottingham Forest
Apr 4 home to Derby
May 7 away at Wolves

Matches They Need to Win
At home: Wolves   Away at: Southend
             Peterborough   Bristol City
             Notts County   Charlton

LUTON

Price Performance

Luton had a good record when the bookmakers wrote off their chances.

They won at their biggest price which was 11/2 at Tranmere.

They also won one of their two matches where they were sent off at 5/1 (away at Wolves).

Luton won three from four at 6/4, but failed to notch a victory in six attempts when priced between 13/8 and 2/1.

Other good priced victories came at 9/4 at Brentford, and at 100/30 at Peterborough.

Results When Odds On

Luton started odds on in five of their matches though they only recorded one win against Oxford.

Somewhat predictably, they drew their shortest priced games at home to Peterborough (4/6) and Bristol Rovers (8/11).

Correct Scores

Luton featured in six 0-0 draws at home, and followed up by drawing four further matches away from home by the same score.

They shared four goals on four occasions, which were evenly split between home and away games.

The two teams that achieved 'the double' over Luton both beat them 4-1 at Kenilworth Road.

First Goalscorer

Gray was easily the best performer for Luton, and he did exceptionally well considering they only scored the first goal in 19 of their matches as a unit. Gray scored seven of them.

Teams They Beat Twice

None

LUTON

Lost Twice To Last Season
Portsmouth   Grimsby

Half-time Comparisons
Luton were leading in 10 matches
They were drawing in 23 matches
And losing in 13 matches
Luton only hung on to five victories from the ten occasions where
they were 'in charge of the game'.
They battled on to force a draw fourteen times after they had
gone in all square.

Significant Number of Goals
Luton failed to score on seventeen occasions, but also kept
sixteen clean sheets. This contributed to a club record, though I
don't care too much for records when they involve a lack of goals.
As a supporter, it would disturb me to find my club scoring more
than two goals in a game just four times throughout the season.
Even then, the net was only hit three times, and on two of those
occasions it was only enough to gain a draw.

Important Games This Season
Aug 14 home to Watford
Aug 21 away at Portsmouth
Oct 9 away at Derby
Dec 18 away at Watford
Jan 22 home to Derby
Feb 22 home to Portsmouth

Matches They Need to Win
At home: Bristol City   Away at: Charlton
              Wolves   Notts County
              Peterborough   Birmingham

MILLWALL

Price Performance

Millwall won at 9/4 (at Charlton) and at 100/30 (at Derby), but they were the only victories in fourteen attempts at prices of 13/8 and above.

They won five times from eight when priced at 11/8, but only one from five when 6/4.

Millwall won on the only occasions they were sent off at 6/5 (beat Notts County 6-0), but lost 1-3 when priced at 11/10 to beat Wolves at Molineux.

Results When Odds On

Millwall were sent off at odds on to beat Birmingham away from home (10/11), but could only manage a draw.

They won nine times from sixteen attempts when odds on at home.

Millwall lost 0-3 at home to Bristol Rovers when playing at their shortest price of 8/15. They also failed to win when made a 4/7 chance to beat Southend.

8/13 was the price to be on as Millwall won four times from five efforts , the game against Barnsley being the exception.

Correct Scores

They lost 0-3 three times away from home, and also drew 1-1 five times on their travels.

There were no obvious ways of making a profit from correct score betting in their home matches.

First Goalscorers

Moralee was the man to be on in this department. Barber also made a significant contribution.

Teams They Beat Twice

Notts County	Derby
Bristol City	Charlton

MILLWALL

Lost Twice To Last Season
(Bristol Rovers)

Half-time Comparisons
Millwall were leading in 17 matches
They were drawing in 13 matches
And losing in 16 matches
Millwall did well to win 13 of the games in which they led at the interval.
Where they lost out was in the drawing situations at the break.
They won just two games from thirteen opportunities, though they lost only three to be fair. Too many matches stayed as they were.
Millwall proved to be great battlers, winning three, and drawing five from half time deficits.

Significant Number of Goals
They failed to score in ten away games and lost in seven in the process.
Millwall allowed the opposition to score more than one goal just five times in their home matches.
They lost by two goals or more eight times which contributed to them missing out on a play-off place at least.

Important Games This Season
Sep 11 away at Charlton
Sep 18 home to Derby
Jan 1 home to Crystal Palace
Mar 12 away at Derby
Mar 16 home to Charlton
Apr 9 away at Crystal Palace

Matches They Need to Win
At home: Birmingham   Away at: Luton
              Southend   Oxford
              Barnsley   Southend

NOTTS COUNTY

Price Performance

Notts County failed to win any of their thirteen games where they started at their biggest prices. This price band ranged from 13/5 to 11/2.

They won three from six when sent off at 11/10, and won their only game at even money at home to Grimsby.

Results When Odds On

Notts County started odds on in just four matches, and they won two of them.

They lost at their shortest price 8/11 (at home to Barnsley), and drew at home to Bristol City at 10/11.

The successes came against Bristol Rovers (5/6) and Southend (10/11).

Correct Scores

Notts County played in two 2-2 draws away from home, and shared six goals at both Bristol Rovers and Grimsby.

They won four games by three goals to one evenly split between home and away.

They lost 0-3 at both Cambridge and at Wolves.

First Goalscorers

Notts County were not the best team to concentrate on for repetitive scorers.

Smith would have given you some sort of run for your money, but otherwise it was best to look at other clubs for involvement.

Teams They Beat Twice

Peterborough

NOTTS COUNTY

Lost Twice To Last Season

Derby   (Newcastle)
Millwall

Half-time Comparisons

Notts County were leading in 11 matches
They were drawing in 19 matches
And losing in 16 matches
County did well to win nine times from their half-time advantage.
They did less than well however, in winning just three times from nineteen drawing situations. They lost seven and drew nine.
County went on to lose ten of the sixteen matches where they were behind, and drew the other six games.

Significant Number of Goals

Only Portsmouth, Luton and Barnsley failed to score against County on their travels.
They scored three goals on seven occasions, winning five of the games and drawing the other two.
They failed to score eleven times away from home which resulted in eight losses.

Important Games This Season

Sep 25 home to Derby
Oct 2 away at Leicester
Oct 30 away at Nottingham Forest
Feb 12 home to Nottingham Forest
Mar 19 away at Derby
Mar 26 home to Leicester

Matches They Need to Win

At home:	Away at:
Luton	Birmingham
Bristol City	Sunderland
Watford	Southend

OXFORD

Price Performance

Oxford had victories at odds of 6/1 (at Derby) and 100/30 (at Wolves). They also achieved a great home win over Newcastle at 15/8.

They won three times from six starts at 15/8, and two wins from three at 7/4.

Oxford only won once from seven attempts in the price band from 11/8 to 13/8, and recorded just one win from five efforts when sent off at 5/4.

Results When Odds On

Oxford started at odds on just five times throughout the season, winning on two occasions.

They won at their shortest price of the year (8/11) when they beat Luton 4-0, they also beat Peterborough at odds of 4/5.

The two that got away at 4/5 were against Southend and Charlton , and Oxford lost both matches by one goal to nil. They also lost to Brentford 0-2 when 5/6 chances.

Correct Scores

Oxford lost six home matches by one goal to nil, but on the other hand they won five games away from home by the same score. On the draw front, they finished level at 1-1 five times away from home, and also shared four goals twice on their travels.

First Goalscorers

Durnin was the star performer in this caregory, though he has since moved on to Portsmouth.

Magilton and Melville contributed well considering Oxford scored first in just nineteen games.

Teams They Beat Twice

(Bristol Rovers)

OXFORD

Lost Twice To Last Season

Sunderland   (Brentford)
Tranmere

Half-time Comparisons

Oxford were leading in 13 matches
They were drawing in 19 matches
And losing in 14 matches
Oxford were obviously driven on by early goals, as they won eleven of the thirteen matches they led in at the break.
By the same token, they lost eleven of the fourteen matches where they were behind.
They let themselves down badly in matches that were all square at the interval.
Oxford won just three times from those 19 opportunities, and lost on seven occasions.

Significant Number of Goals

Oxford failed to score in eleven home matches. However, they did restrict the opposition to a maximum of one goal nineteen times at the Manor Ground.
They scored a single goal in fourteen matches away from home.
Oxford conceded just eight goals in the second half in their collective home games.

Important Games This Season

Aug 14 home to Portsmouth
Sep 4 away at Nottingham Forest
Nov 13 home to Derby
Dec 18 away at Portsmouth
Feb 26 home to Nottingham Forest
Apr 30 away at Derby

Matches They Need to Win

At home: Sunderland   Away at: Bristol City
             Birmingham   Birmingham
             Southend   Luton

PETERBOROUGH

Price Performance

Either the bookmakers got it wrong, or Peterborough ignored the rules when playing supposed superior opposition.

Peterborough won seven games from nine when priced between 9/5 and 9/4.

They then went on to record victories at 3/1 (at Charlton), 7/2 (at Derby) and at 4/1 (at Leicester). They failed at their four biggest prices, but by then they had proved their point.

In contrast, they failed to win a game when they were sent off between Evens and 5/4 which they did on six occasions.

Results When Odds On

Peterborough started at odds on ten times, but only managed to win four of them.

They only drew with Bristol Rovers when 8/13 chances (their shortest price), and also drew both matches when priced at 4/5 against Oxford and Watford.

Correct Scores

Peterborough featured in seven 1-1 draws at home. They also shared six goals with Swindon in front of their own fans.

They lost to the odd goal in five on two occasions away from home.

First Goalscorers

Peterborough did well to score the first goal of the game twenty two times. This was reflected in the impressive list of scorers in this department.

Adcock was top of the tree, but Philiskirk and to a lesser degree Sterling, gave good support.

Teams They Beat Twice

Derby
Southend
Grimsby
Leicester

PETERBOROUGH

Lost Twice To Last Season

Notts County
(West Ham)
(Newcastle)
Wolves

Half-time Comparisons

Peterborough were leading in 15 matches
They were drawing in 19 matches
And losing in 12 matches
On the negative side, Peterborough lost 11 of the 12 games when they were behind at the break. They held on to win 11 when in front though, and drew the other four.
They won and lost five times when going in all square at the break. That left nine games that remained a draw at the death.

Significant Number of Goals

Although 'The Posh' did well to score in 19 of their 23 home games, they only found the net once on thirteen occasions.
Peterborough also conceded three goals five times in front of their own supporters.

Important Games This Season

Sep 11 away at Derby
Oct 16 away at West Brom
Nov 13 away at Nottingham Forest
Jan 15 home to West Brom
Mar 15 home to Derby
Apr 30 home to Nottingham Forest

Matches They Need To Win

At home: Notts County
             Barnsley
             Watford
Away at: Sunderland
             Luton
             Notts County

PORTSMOUTH

Price Performance

Portsmouth won at Derby when priced at 100/30. The only time they were a bigger price was when they travelled to Newcastle. They lost 1-3 at odds of 9/2.

They only won one match out of 15 when their price ranged from 7/4 to 13/5, which was at Luton where they won 4-1 at odds of 2/1. Portsmouth were absolute bankers when fancied by the bookmakers. They were one team that you could totally rely on to do the business.

They won ten matches from twelve when starting between 13/8 and even money.

Results When Odds On

Portsmouth only started odds on in their matches at home, but what inspired performances they were.

They were odds on on seventeen occasions and duly obliged in fourteen of them.

They were in the meanest form when priced between 8/11 and 8/13. They won all nine of the games they played in this price band.

Correct Scores

Portsmouth won 4-0 on three occasions in front of their home supporters, and won another five by the only goal of the game. They shared six goals at Bristol City on the opening day of the season, and split ten goals with Oxford at The Manor.

First Goalscorers

Portsmouth scored the first goal 29 times from 43 games where goals were scored.

Guy Whittingham was obviously the man to follow, and opened the scoring on no less than ten occasions.

Whittingham had marvellous support from McLoughlin who more than paid his way, scoring six times in this department.

Teams They Beat Twice

Birmingham	(Cambridge)	Tranmere
(Bristol Rovers)	Luton	Derby

PORTSMOUTH

Lost Twice To Last Season
(West Ham)

Half-time Comparisons
Portsmouth were leading in 20 matches
They were drawing in 17 matches
And losing in 9 matches
Portsmouth were devastating when in front at half time. They won seventeen of the twenty they led in, and won all thirteen games at home where they led at the break.
They only managed to save two games when behind though, grabbing a draw at Luton after being two down, and actually winning against Grimsby at Fratton Park.
They managed to turn eight of the drawing situations into victories, and lost just three.

Significant Number of Goals
In an amazing season in front of their home supporters, Portsmouth only failed to score twice (West Ham & Notts County), and stopped their opponents from scoring 16 times in 23 games. They conceded more than one goal just once, when they lost 2-3 to Bristol City.

Important Games This Season
Oct 2 away at Nottingham Forest
Oct 16 home to Derby
Jan 3 home to Leicester
Jan 15 away at Derby
Mar 26 home to Nottingham Forest
Mar 30 away at Leicester

Matches They Need To Win
At home: Notts County
           Bristol City
           Leicester
Away at: Bristol City
           Watford
           Peterborough

SOUTHEND

Price Performance

Southend started at 7/2 twice during the season, and they won both the games against Bristol City and Sunderland.

They started at even bigger prices in eight more matches, but failed to win.

Southend only managed two wins from six games when sent off at 6/5, and failed to win in three attempts at 5/4.

Results When Odds On

Southend only went off at odds on twice, and they won both matches.

They were 8/11 when they beat Bristol Rovers by three goals to nil, and 4/5 when defeating Luton 2-1.

Correct Scores

Southend drew five home matches 1-1, and managed three 3-0 victories at Roots Hall.

They lost 0-2 four times on their travels, and by the odd goal in five on two occasions.

First Goalscorers

Collymore was the obvious candidate for Southend on the scoring front, and he did not let his followers down. Of the five times he scored the opening goals, three of them were away from home, which is usually the sign of a good striker. How Nottingham Forest could have quibbled about a few thousand for a player of this potential I do not know. They have lived to regret such actions.

Teams They Beat Twice

(Bristol Rovers)

SOUTHEND

Lost Twice To Last Season

Peterborough   Tranmere

Half-time Comparisons

Southend were leading in 8 matches
They were drawing in 23 matches
And losing in 15 matches
As you can see, Southend only led in eight matches all year at the interval, and all of those were at home. They went on to win seven of them.
They only managed to win five of the games where they were level, and lost eight.
Southend lost eleven of the fifteen where they trailed at half-time.

Significant Number of Goals

Southend scored just five goals in the first half of their collective away matches. This equates to a goal every 207 minutes, or once every three and a half hours.
On the positive side, they did manage another 16 goals in the second half of those games.
They managed to score a maximum of one goal in 33 of their 46 matches. Obviously they need to improve significantly if they have any hope of beating relegation again.

Important Games This Season

Sep 18 away at Portsmouth
Nov 27 away at Derby
Dec 28 away at Crystal Palace
Mar 12 home to Portsmouth
Apr 6 home to Crystal Palace
May 7 home to Derby

Matches They Need To Win

At home: Peterborough   Away at: Barnsley
            Watford   Peterborough
            Bristol City   Notts County

SUNDERLAND

Price Performance

Sunderland's biggest price of the season was 5/1. They won at Derby, but lost at Newcastle, one goal being enough to settle the issue in both games.

They ranged from 2/1 to 13/5 eight times without winning, and only managed five wins from fifteen attempts when competing in the price band of 11/10 and 13/8.

On the plus side, they won two from three when sent off warm favourites at even money. The exception being the match they lost to Birmingham at Roker Park.

Results When Odds On

Their performances when odds on were less than impressive it must be said.

Eight times they were made odds on and they only beat Tranmere and Grimsby.

They lost all four of their shortest priced matches (4/5 to 4/6), the two successful games came at 10/11.

Correct Scores

High scoring draws were a feature at Roker Park, when they shared four goals with both Notts County and Luton. They played in a 3-3 draw with Cambridge for which they started at 8/11.

They lost 1-2 eight times in all, and lost by the only goal of the game four times on their travels.

First Goalscorers

Goodman saved Sunderland's blushes by scoring the opening goal on six occasions. Considering Sunderland only scored first 17 times as a unit, Goodman did a remarkable job.

Teams They Beat Twice

Oxford
Derby

SUNDERLAND

Lost Twice To Last Season

(Newcastle)	Leicester	Watford
(Swindon)	Birmingham	

Half-time Comparisons

Sunderland were leading in 12 matches
They were drawing in 23 matches
And losing in eleven matches
Sunderland only converted seven of their positive interval scores into victories.
Of the twenty three games that were level, they won six, drew five and lost twelve. The warning lights are flashing with those stats.
Sunderland salvaged two draws from the eleven games in which they trailed, and lost the rest.

Significant Number of Goals

Seventeen of Sunderland's games were without goals by half-time, and eight of those were at home. A more positive approach is obviously needed.
They also failed to score at all in ten away games.

Important Games This Season

Aug 14 away at Derby
Oct 16 away at Middlesbrough
Nov 6 home to Portsmouth
Dec 4 away at Portsmouth
Dec 18 home to Derby
Jan 15 home to Middlesbrough

Matches They Need To Win

At home:	Notts County	Away at:	Birmingham
	Watford		Barnsley
	Birmingham		Notts County

TRANMERE

Price Performance

Tranmere won at 11/4 and 3/1 at Leicester and Derby respectively. Their biggest prices of the season were 4/1 and 9/2 and they lost both games.

They were priced at 11/8 eight times, and won half of them. Pricing Tranmere at 11/8 so often is a good illustration of just how difficult this league is.

They won their only game at even money against Sunderland, and also won at 7/4 away at Oxford.

Results When Odds On

Tranmere started odds on fifteen times and won ten of them. They had a good record at 4/6 when they won all three games, and were victorious twice in three starts at 10/11. The match they lost was when they entertained Leicester.

Correct Scores

They beat both Birmingham and Oxford by four goals to nil at Prenton Park, and also won 2-1 on another five occasions.

Tranmere beat Southend, Wolves and Bristol City by three goals to nil at home.

First Goalscorers

John Aldridge continued his quest for goals and once again came up with the goods.

Nevin and Morrissey also contributed to the cause in good fashion.

Teams They Beat Twice

(Cambridge)
Bristol City
Southend
(Brentford)
Oxford
Derby
Wolves

TRANMERE

Lost Twice To Last Season
(Newcastle)   Portsmouth

Half-time Comparisons
Tranmere were leading in 14 matches
They were drawing in 19 matches
And losing in 13 matches
Tranmere went on to win eleven of those fourteen matches, and drew the other three.
They had a better record than most in the drawing and losing situations at half time.
Tranmere won eight games for instance, from the nineteen they were drawing in, and turned four of the thirteen losing situations into victories.

Significant Number of Goals
Tranmere scored at least two goals on no less than sixteen occasions at home.
They failed to score nine times on their travels, and only scored one on six other occasions.
Tranmere won twelve games by a single goal, and eleven by two goals or more.

Important Games This Season
Oct 9 home to Bolton
Oct 16 away at Nottingham Forest
Jan 3 away at Derby
Jan 15 home to Nottingham Forest
Jan 22 away at Bolton
Mar 29 home to Derby

Matches They Need to Win
At home: Peterborough
             Millwall
             Luton
Away at: Sunderland
             Watford
             Charlton

WATFORD

Price Performance

Watford won at 9/2 (at Derby), but failed in nine other games when priced 11/4 or more.

They also won only three from thirteen when priced between 11/10 and 13/8.

Watford won both games when sent off at 9/5 (home to Wolves and away at Barnsley), and also when priced at 2/1 against Newcastle at home and Notts County away.

Results When Odds On

The bookmakers were not too impressed with Watford, and only sent them off at odds on twice.

They beat Bristol Rovers 4-2 at odds of 8/11, but could only draw with Cambridge when 4/5.

Correct Scores

Watford featured in five 0-0 draws at Vicarage Road, but they did beat both Millwall and Leicester by three goals to one.

They lost by the odd goal in five to Grimsby at home, and to Grimsby away.

They lost 2-5 at both Leicester and Millwall.

First Goalscorers

Furlong was the man in charge for Watford, and he received good support from Charlery.

Teams They Beat Twice

Sunderland
(Bristol Rovers)

WATFORD

Lost To Twice Last Season

Leicester   Grimsby
(West Ham)   (Swindon)

Half-Time Comparisons

Watford were leading in 14 matches
They were drawing in 19 matches
And losing in 13 matches
Watford let six of their interval advantages slip away by drawing four and losing two after being in front at the break.
They won five from nineteen after being all-square, and lost seven with seven remaining level.
Watford lost ten of the thirteen when they were behind, but did manage one win at Southend.

Significant Number of Goals

Only Barnsley, Bristol Rovers and Peterborough failed to score against Watford when they left Vicarage Road.
Watford only failed to score four times away from home (Newcastle, Luton, Peterborough and Portsmouth) which is very commendable.
Unfortunately though, it happened eight times in front of their own supporters.

Important Games This Season

Aug 14 away at Luton
Oct 2 away at Millwall
Nov 27 home to Crystal Palace
Dec 18 home to Luton
Mar 26 home to Millwall
May 7 away at Crystal Palace

Matches They Need to Win

At home: Luton   Away at: Birmingham
            Southend   Peterborough
            Oxford   Luton

WOLVES

Price Performance

Wolves failed to win in their five matches where they started at extended odds which ranged from 3/1 to 8/1.

They did beat Charlton though when priced up at 13/5.

Their worst record came in the games where they started at 6/4. Such matches should be hard fought affairs with the result possibly going either way. The games certainly went the wrong way for Wolves as they won just once in six efforts.

Results When Odds On

Wolves won six from fourteen when sent off at odds on by the bookmakers.

They lost at home to Luton at their shortest price of the season which was 4/7.

Wolves only won twice from six attempts when 8/11 chances. They also won two from three when they were 10/11, the exception being when they drew at home to Portsmouth.

Correct Scores

Wolves shared four goals at home to both Swindon and Watford early on in the season.

They lost 0-2 four times on their travels, but won 2-1 four times at home.

Wolves beat both Leicester and Notts County by three goals to nil at Molineux.

First Goalscorers

Steve Bull was predictably the chief contributor, and he did well considering he suffered from injury for a fair part of the season. Dennison and Mutch also played their part in a generally disappointing season.

Teams They Beat Twice

Peterborough
Charlton
Birmingham
Barnsley

112

WOLVES

Lost To Twice Last Season
Derby
Tranmere

Half-Time Comparisons
Wolves were leading in 9 matches
They were drawing in 28 matches
And losing in 9 matches
Something tells me that Wolves are going to have to adopt a more positive approach.
Their manager desperately needs promotion this time around, and the pre-season transfer business suggests that it is now or never.
Wolves went on to win seven of those nine games that they led in, and lost seven of the nine they trailed in.
They managed only eight victories from the twenty eight games where they were level, and improvement has to come in this department.

Significant Number of Goals
Wolves were involved in twenty matches that reached the half way stage without a goal being scored by either club.
They managed a maximum of one goal nineteen times away from home, with ten matches producing none.
Wolves lost seven matches away from home by two goals or more.

Important Games This Season
Aug 21 away at Birmingham
Sep 4 away at West Brom
Nov 6 away at Derby
Dec 4 home to Derby
Feb 22 home to Birmingham
Feb 26 home to West Brom

Matches They Need to Win

At home:	Watford	Away at:	Oxford
	Luton		Notts County
	Bristol City		Bristol City

Second Division

BLACKPOOL

Price Performance

Blackpool won at their biggest price of the season when they won at Stoke at the rewarding odds of 9/1.

They failed to win in another ten attempts when priced at 100/30 or more.

There were still some good prices to be had when they won at 3/1 (at Exeter) and 13/5 (at Chester).

At the other end of the market, Blackpool disappointed when only winning three from eleven when either 11/8 or 6/4.

Results when odds on

Blackpool won three of the six games when they started odds on.

They won at their shortest price of 4/7 at home to Chester, but could only draw with Mansfield when 4/6 chances.

Their other two victories came at 8/11 (Exeter) and 5/6 (Wigan).

Correct Scores

Blackpool drew five home matches 1-1, and won another five by two goals to nil.

They shared four goals four times with an even split between home and away.

Blackpool also drew 3-3 at Preston.

First Goalscorers

Eyres, Bamber and Sinclair all did well for 'The Seasiders'.

Sinclair's goals included three away from home, which helped Blackpool to win seven points in those games.

Teams they beat twice

(Chester)
Exeter

BLACKPOOL

Lost to twice last season
Port Vale

Half-time Comparisons
Blackpool were leading in 12 matches
They were drawing in eighteen matches
And losing in sixteen matches
Blackpool duly lost 13 of the sixteen that they trailed in at the break, and won seven of the matches where they were in front. Like most other teams, it was the drawing situations that dictated their season, and they won just four from eighteen which ensured a struggle for survival.

Significant number of goals
Only Reading and Swansea prevented Blackpool from scoring at Bloomfield Road.
Unfortunately they only managed a single goal in another seven matches at home, and did not win any of those games.
Only four teams failed to score against Blackpool when they played away, and this contributed towards just 3 wins.

Important games this season
Aug 21 home to Brentford
Oct 16 home to Port Vale
Dec 11 away at Brentford
Dec 27 away at Stockport
Jan 15 away at Port Vale
Apr 2 home to Stockport

Matches they need to win
At home: Huddersfield
            Plymouth
            Hartlepool

Away at: Reading
            Hull
            Bournemouth

BOURNEMOUTH

Price Performance

Bournemouth had one victory at 7/2 at Bradford City. This was their only success from twelve attempts when priced at 3/1 or more.

They played five games in the price band from 11/10 to 5/4, and failed to win any of them.

They won two from five at 6/4, and one from five at 13/8.

Results when odds on

Bournemouth won three times from the nine in which they started odds on.

Their shortest price all season was 8/13 which they started at on three occasions. They failed to win any of them.

Bournemouth's successes came at 4/6, 8/11 and 5/6.

Correct Scores

Bournemouth played in ten 1-1 draws which were evenly split home and away.

They also drew 0-0 four times at home, and lost 0-3 at both Hull and Port Vale.

First Goalscorers

McGorry was Bournemouth's hero, not only because he scored the first goal in five matches, but also because those goals set up victory in every match.

Ekoku did extremely well before moving on to Norwich.

Teams they beat twice

(Mansfield)

BOURNEMOUTH

Lost twice to

Swansea
(West Brom)
Plymouth

Half-time Comparisons

Bournemouth were leading in twelve matches
They were drawing in twenty-two
And losing in twelve
Bournemouth let ten points slip away when they allowed winning situations to turn into draws.
They lost eleven of the twelve matches they were behind in, and won only five from the 22 where they were level.

Significant number of goals

Bournemouth only managed to score more than one goal in a match on nine occasions
They lost ten games by a single goal, another seven by two goals or more.
Bournemouth conceded a single goal twenty one times in all, so it came as no surprise when they featured in so many 'jackpot' draws.

Important games this season

Oct 16 home to Brighton
Nov 2 home to Port Vale
Dec 27 home to Brentford
Jan 15 away at Brighton
Apr 2 away at Brentford
Apr 16 away at Port Vale

Matches they need to win

At home: Huddersfield
           Hull
           Plymouth
Away at: Blackpool
           Plymouth
           Hull

BRADFORD CITY

Price Performance

Bradford won at 4/1 in a tough looking fixture at Port Vale.
They started at 5/2 or more on another nine occasions without winning.
Bradford won four from six when sent off at 6/4, and they won the only time they started at 6/5 which was at home to Stockport.

Results when odds on

Bradford started odds on fifteen times and they won seven of them.
They lost to Hartlepool when they were 2/5 (shortest price of the season), and won three from five when priced at 5/6.
Bradford also failed to win when sent off as very warm favourites at 4/7 and 4/6.

Correct Scores

Anybody wanting to make a profit out of Bradford's matches should have looked to the away draws.
They shared six goals with Blackpool, they shared four with both Stockport and Burnley, and they drew 1-1 five times into the bargain. They also won 3-1 three times at home.

First Goalscorers

McCarthey stood out for prospective punters, whilst Jewell and Reid paid their way.

Teams they beat twice

(Wigan)
Port Vale
(Chester)
Exeter

BRADFORD CITY

Lost to twice last season
Rotherham
Hartlepool

Half-time Comparisons
Bradford were leading in twelve matches
They were drawing in twenty matches
And losing in fourteen matches
They won ten of the games in which they led, and lost nine of the fourteen where they were behind at the interval.
Bradford won six of the twenty where they were all-square, and lost five of them.

Significant number of goals
Only Hull, Exeter and Bournemouth failed to score against Bradford when they played away from home.
They won eleven games by a single goal.
Bradford scored three goals six times at home, and naturally enough won all the games.

Important games this season
Oct 16 home to Burnley
Nov 2 home Huddersfield
Jan 3 away at Port Vale
Jan 15 away at Burnley
Mar 29 home to Port Vale
Apr 16 away at Huddersfield

Matches they need to win
At home: Bournemouth
              Plymouth
              Hartlepool

Away at: Hartlepool
              Blackpool
              Burnley

BRIGHTON

Price Performance

Brighton were well respected by the bookies, and their largest price all season was only 7/2. They won at Bolton at that price, but lost at West Brom.

They also started at 3/1 twice, and again won one of the matches (Swansea) and drew the other at Stockport.

Results when odds on

Brighton just scraped home by three goals to two against Chester when playing at their shortest price of the season which was 2/5.

They won three of the four games when they were sent off at 4/5, and two of the four at 8/11.

Brighton only won once from four attempts when priced up at 10/11.

Correct Scores

They lost 2-3 twice on their travels at Plymouth and Leyton Orient, and won 3-2 at home against Chester and away at Exeter.

They also won 3-1 four times, twice at home and twice away.

First Goalscorers

Nogan was in supreme form for Brighton, and local bookmakers would have caught a severe cold if they laid him to level stakes. Foster contributed as always.

Teams they beat twice

Exeter
(Mansfield)
Huddersfield
(Bolton)
(Wigan)
Burnley

BRIGHTON

Lost to twice last season

Reading   Fulham   Leyton Orient
Port Vale   Rotherham

Half-time Comparisons

Brighton were leading in twelve matches
They were drawing in twenty-two matches
And losing in twelve
Brighton won all twelve games where they found themselves in front at the interval. They won eight times at home and four away.
They lost nine of the twelve games where they trailed, and both won and lost eight games from their 22 drawing situations.

Significant Number of Goals

Only Swansea, Bolton and Stockport failed to score against Brighton on their travels.
To Brighton's credit though, they themselves only failed to score four times in front of their home supporters.
Brighton both won and lost nine times by two goals or more.

Important Games This Season

Sep 18 home to Brentford
Oct 16 away at Bournemouth
Nov 27 away at Port Vale
Jan 15 home to Bournemouth
Mar 12 away at Brentford
May 7 home to Port Vale

Matches they need to win

At home: Reading
            Hartlepool
            Blackpool

Away at: Blackpool
            Hull
            Plymouth

BURNLEY

Price Performance

Burnley's biggest priced win was at Rotherham where they started at 100/30. They only started one match at a larger price, and that was when they played Stoke and went off at 5/1.

They only won three games from seventeen efforts when priced at 7/4 or more.

Burnley won both their games against Leyton Orient and Mansfield on the two occasions they started at even money. They won just once from eleven attempts when their price ranged from 11/10 and 6/4. That win came against Fulham at odds of 5/4.

Results when odds on

Burnley started odds on thirteen times, and won seven of them. They won all five matches when priced between 1/2 and 4/6 which were the shortest on offer all season.

Burnley started at 8/11 twice and 10/11 on two occasions, but could manage only three draws and a defeat from the four games.

Correct Scores

The correct score to be on was 1-1. Burnley drew eleven matches sharing two goals, with six of them coming away from home.

Burnley also played in two 2-2 draws at Turf Moor.

They were on the receiving end of two 0-4 defeats at the hands of Bolton and Fulham.

First Goalscorers

Heath had his name up in lights again having had another good season.

He received good support from Harper.

Teams they beat twice

Hull

BURNLEY

Lost to twice last season

(Bolton)   Brighton

Half-time Comparisons

Burnley were leading in 17 matches
They were drawing in 15 matches
And losing in 14 matches
Cause for concern centered on the drawing situations again.
Burnley won just three games from the fifteen where they were
level in at Half-time.
Of the games where they led at the interval, Burnley won twelve
and drew five. They lost eleven of the fourteen games where they
were behind.

Significant number of goals

Only Hull, Rotherham and Hartlepool failed to score against
Burnley when they played away from home.
Burnley failed to score in ten away games, and scored just one
goal in a further eight matches.
They did restrict the opposition to a maximum of one goal on
eighteen occasions at Turf Moor.

Important games this season

Aug 14 home to Port Vale
Sep 18 away at Stockport
Oct 16 away at Bradford City
Dec 18 away at Port Vale
Jan 15 home to Bradford City
Mar 12 home to Stockport

Matches they need to win

At home: Plymouth
             Bournemouth
             Blackpool

Away at: Exeter
             Huddersfield
             Stockport

EXETER

Price Performance

Exeter won at 4/1 on two occasions last season. Both matches were away, beating both Hartlepool and Bournemouth by the same score of 3-1.

They started four other matches at even bigger odds but failed to win any of them.

Exeter won two of the four matches they played when priced at 6/4, but only one from six when 11/8 chances.

They played five matches in the price band between evens and 5/4 and never won a game.

Results when odds on

Exeter won just three of the seven games they started at odds on. They beat Chester 2-0 at their shortest price of 8/11, and other successes came at 4/5 and 10/11 against Hartlepool and Mansfield respectively.

Exeter played three other games at odds of 10/11, and lost to Preston and Huddersfield while they drew with Hull.

Correct Scores

The 2-2 draw was the score to be on in Exeter's games. They shared four goals six times throughout the season, three at home and three away.

They also lost to the odd goal in five at home to both West Brom and Brighton.

First Goalscorer

Moran, Jepson and Whiston all gave good accounts of themselves through the season.

Teams they beat twice

Hartlepool
(Chester)
Plymouth

EXETER

Lost to twice last season

Brighton   (Bolton)   (West Brom)
Blackpool   Bradford City

Half-time comparisons

Exeter were leading in 11 matches
They were drawing in 20 matchs
And losing in 15 matches
Exeter salvaged five draws from the matches where they were
behind at the break.
They managed seven wins from the eleven games where they
led, but only four from the twenty drawing opportunities.

Significant number of goals

Exeter featured in fifteen goal-less first halves, with ten of them
coming in home matches
They lost seven games by a single goal and another eleven by two
goals or more. This might suggest that another struggle against
relegation is on the cards.

Important games this season

Aug 14 away at Brentford
Sep 15 away at Bristol Rovers
Nov 20 home to Port Vale
Mar 15 home to Bristol Rovers
Dec 18 home to Brentford
Apr 30 away at Port Vale

Matches they need to win

At home: Burnley
           Blackpool
           Hull

Away at: Huddersfield
           Hull
           Blackpool

FULHAM

Price Performance

Fulham's biggest priced win was at 100/30 when they won at Brighton.

Their priced ranged from 2/1 to 6/1 eleven times, but the victory at Brighton was their only success in this price band.

Fulham only won once from five starts when they were well fancied to win. They beat Burnley 4-0 at odds of 11/10, but failed at evens (twice), 6/5 and 5/4.

They won three times from eight attempts at 6/4, but won two from three at 7/4 the exception being at Burnley where they went down 2-5.

Results at odds on

Fulham were one of the few teams to start an away match at odds on. This was at Chester where they won 3-2 at odds of 10/11.

They won five matches out of nine at home when odds on, their winning prices being 4/6, 8/11, 5/6 and 10/11 (twice). They also failed at 4/6 and 8/11. They lost to Huddersfield at 5/6 and drew with Swansea at 10/11 .

Correct Scores

Fulham drew 1-1 in five home matches, and also featured in the jackpot draw four times on their travels.

They shared six goals at home to Hull, and also won with the only goal of the game four times at Craven Cottage.

First Goalscorers

Nothing to write home about here really, though Eckhardt and Farrell did well enough.

Brazil would also have given you a run for your money.

Teams they beat twice

(Wigan)
Brighton
(Preston)
(Chester)

FULHAM

Lost to twice last season
(Bolton)
Huddersfield

Half-time comparisons
Fulham were leading in twelve matches
They were drawing in 21 matches
And losing in thirteen matches
Fulham lost just six of the matches where they trailed at half-time. They drew six matches after being behind, and won at Preston having been a goal down for over three quarters of an hour.
They won nine of the matches where they led, and managed 26 points from a possible 63 where they went in level at the break.

Significant number of goals
Fulham scored a maximum of one goal 17 times at home which was disappointing.
They won ten games by a single goal, and a further half dozen by two goals or more.

Important games this season
Oct 2 home to Leyton Orient
Dec 27 home to Port Vale
Jan 1 home to Brentford
Mar 26 away at Leyton Orient
Apr 2 away at Port Vale
Apr 9 away at Brentford

Matches they need to win

At home:		Away at:	
	Hull		Bournemouth
	Huddersfield		Burnley
	Exeter		Huddersfield

HARTLEPOOL

Price percentage

Hartlepool won both matches against Stockport and Huddersfield when starting at 5/4.

At the other end of the market, they beat Stoke away at 8/1. They also won when priced at 9/2 to beat Bradford City.

They won just two from seven when priced between even money and 6/5.

Hartlepool gained just one point from the three matches where they started at 6/4.

Results when odds on

Hartlepool's record was less than impressive when the bookmakers fancied them to win. They won just three from eight when odds on.

Hartlepool scored only six goals in those eight games.

The three games they won only totalled a winning aggregate of 4 goals to nil.

For the record they won at 8/13, 4/6 and 4/5.

Correct Scores

Hartlepool played in two 2-2 draws away from home. They were at Wigan and Plymouth.

They won by the only goal of the game four times at home, and lost 0-3 at Huddersfield Swansea and Burnley.

First Goalscorer

Saville and Johnrose contributed, but generally this was not Hartlepool's strong point. They need a striker who can set them on their way more often.

Teams they beat twice

Bradford City

HARTLEPOOL

Lost to twice last season

Swansea   Exeter
(Mansfield)

Half-time comparisons

Hartlepool were leading in ten matches
They were drawing in twenty-five matches
And losing in eleven matches
Hartlepool went on to win eight of the games where they were in front, but lost ten of the eleven where they were behind. They were adrift in six matches at home by half-time, and they lost them all.

Significant number of goals

Hartlepool were involved in nineteen matches which had not produced a goal by half-time.
It follows therefore, that they failed to score in nineteen of their forty six matches.
Hartlepool managed to score just seven first half goals in front of their own supporters.
On the positive side, they did manage to keep sixteen clean sheets.

Importat games this season

Sep 18 away at Port Vale
Sep 25 home to York
Oct 9 home to Brentford
Jan 22 away at Brentford
Mar 12 home to Port Vale
Mar 19 away at York

Matches they need to win

At home:	Blackpool	Away at:	Plymouth
	Exeter		Blackpool
	Bournemouth		Exeter

HUDDERSFIELD

Price Performance

Huddersfield were the team to be on when they were priced at 100/30. They won three times from six attampts. Their victories came at Plymouth, Bradford and Mansfield.

They started at a bigger price on seven occasions but failed to record a victory.

Huddersfield won just two from eight when chalked up at 6/4, whilst they won two from five at 13/8.

They did win both games when sent off at even money, beating Blackpool and Mansfield.

Results when odds on

Huddersfield only started at odds on four times throughout the season. They won two of the four.

Their victories came against Wigan (4/6) and Hull (5/6), whilst they drew with Exeter and lost to Chester,having been priced up at 10/11 for both matches.

Correct Scores

Huddersfield drew 2-2 at both West Brom and Blackpool.

They lost 1-2 eight times during the season, with four of the losses coming at home.

Huddersfield were invloved in four jackpot draws at Leeds Road, whilst they beat Hull and Hartlepool by three goals to nil.

First Goalscorer

Nothing to write home about here, though O'Regan and Barnett kept the goals ticking over without necessarily making a profit for their followers.

Teams they beat twice

Hull
Plymouth
(Mansfield)
Fulham

HUDDERSFIELD

Lost to twice last season
Swansea   Port Vale   Brighton

Half-time Comparisons
Huddersfield were leading in 8 matches
They were drawing in twenty-one matches
And losing in seventeen matches
They won seven of the eight games when they were in front at the interval, the exception being when they lost to Bradford.
Huddersfield did well to win nine games from the 21 they were drawing in, whilst they lost 13 of the 17 where they were behind at the break.

Significant number of goals
Huddersfield were one of only two clubs who failed to score at home against Chester.
They only scored the first goal of the game fifteen times, so thus faced an uphill struggle having been behind in 29 matches.
Huddersfield only featured in two scoreless games all season, which were both at home against Reading and Exeter.

Important games this season
Aug 28 home to Stockport
Sep 14 home to Port Vale
Nov 27 home to Brentford
Feb 19 away at Stockport
Mar 15 away at Port Vale
May 7 away at Brentford

Matches they need to win
At home: Reading
            Exeter
            Bournemouth

Away at: Hartlepool
            Bournemouth
            Blackpool

HULL

Price Performance

Hull won at Rotherham when priced at 4/1. They played two matches at bigger prices without success.

They had another good priced victory at Bradford when sent off at 100/30, they failed to record a win in eleven matches when priced between 9/4 and 3/1.

Hull won only two from six at 11/8, but won two from three at 7/4, the exception being when they lost at home to Port Vale.

Results when odds on

Hull started odds on ten times, which is rather surprising for a team that avoided relegation by the skin of their teeth.

You could not argue with the results though, as Hull enjoyed a fifty per cent success rate. They won all five games at home naturally, and the victims were Swansea (10/11), Blackpool (10/11), Mansfield (5/6), Hartlepool (8/11), and Bournemouth at 10/11.

They failed at 8/11, 10/11 and 5/6 three times, losing three of them and drawing twice.

Correct Scores

Hull shared six goals at Fulham, and lost 0-2 away on four occasions.

They beat both Blackpool and Hartlepool 3-2 at home, and also won four games by the only goal of the game at Boothferry Park.

First Goalscorers

Hunter was the man to follow, particularly in home matches. Atkinson also gave a helping hand to Hull's cause.

Teams they beat twice

Nil

HULL

Lost to twice last season

Huddersfield	Burnley	Stockport
(Bolton)	(West Brom)	

Half-time Comparisons

Hull were leading in eleven matches
They were drawing in nineteen matches
And losing in sixteen matches
Hull let five games slip when they were in front at the break, winning six matches.
They had a fair record in games that were all square at the interval, winning six and losing six of the 19 matches.
Predictably enough, their major problems occured when they were behind. They went on to lose 14 of those 16 matches.

Significant number of goals

Hull lost 11 of their 13 away defeats by two goals or more.
They conceded just seven goals in the first half of their collective home games. Sorry to relate that 19 more goals were conceded in the second half.

Important Games this Season

Aug 31 home to Brentford
Oct 9 away at Port Vale
Nov 27 home to Stockport
Jan 22 home to Port Vale
Feb 22 away at Brentford
May 7 away to Stockport

Matches they need to win

At home:	Rotherham
	Huddersfield
	Burnley
Away at:	Hartlepool
	Plymouth
	Huddersfield

LEYTON ORIENT

Price Performance

Orient won their only two games when priced at 13/5, at Brighton and Swansea.

They also won at 9/4 at Hartlepool, but failed to record a win in nine other games where they were 7/4 or more.

They only won once from five attempts at 6/4 (home to Stoke), but won all four when priced at either Evens or 11/10. They beat Blackpool and Brighton when 'levels', and Stockport and Bradford at 'tips'.

Results when odds on

Orient won ten games from 16 when they started at odds on. They lost at their shortest price of the season (1/2 against Wigan), but won all four matches when priced between 8/13 and 8/15.

They won both games at 10/11 and two from three at 4/5, the exception being when they featured in a scoreless draw at home to Hull.

Correct Scores

Orient beat both Burnley and Brighton 3-2 at Brisbane Road, and also won 1-0 four times at home.

They won 3-1 at both Chester and Brighton, and drew 1-1 four times on their travels.

Orient lost 1-3 at both Blackpool and Wigan.

First Goalscorers

Taylor led the way with Otto hot on his heels.

Both players would have made a profit for you, and Bellamy chipped in with a contribution as well.

Teams they beat twice

(Chester)
Brighton
(Preston)
Swansea

LEYTON ORIENT

Lost to twice last season
Port Vale   (Wigan)

Half-time Comparisons
Orient were leading in 18 matches
They were drawing in twenty matches
And losing in eight matches
They won 16 of the 18 games where they were in front, dropping just four points in the process.
For a team that was beaten by goal difference for a place in the play-offs, their record in matches that were level at the interval was atrocious. They won just four games from 20 when level at the break, and managed to lose ten.

Significant number of goals
The five goals that Orient conceded to Wigan will haunt them. Orient were the only club that Wigan beat twice all season.
Orient failed to score in eleven games away from home, and in those matches only Hull, Hartlepool and Swansea failed to score against them.
They scored the opening goal in an impressive 24 games, and only lost once when doing so at Stoke.

Important Games this Season
Sep 14 away at Brentford
Sep 18 home to Barnet
Oct 2 away at Fulham
Mar 12 away at Barnet
Mar 15 home to Brentford
Mar 26 home to Fulham

Matches they need to win

At home:	Hull	Away at:	Blackpool
	Hartlepool		Exeter
	Reading		Plymouth

PLYMOUTH

Price Performance

Plymouth upset the form book at odds of 11/2 when they won at West Brom.

That was their only victory in twelve though when priced at 9/4 or more.

Plymouth won two games from five when 6/4 chances, and won just two from seven between 11/8 and Evens.

They played four matches when marginally rated second best at 13/8, and lost three of the four games.

Results when odds on

Plymouth's record when odds on was impressive. They won two thirds of their games when fancied by the bookmakers.

They won at their shortest price of 8/15, and all 3 at 4/5. They beat Blackpool and Bradford at 5/6, and the only prices they failed at were 8/11 and 10/11 three times.

Correct Scores

Plymouth features in four 0-0 draws away from home. (Peter Shilton's influence no doubt).

They shared four goals against Hartlepool and Reading at home, and also drew 2-2 at Rotherham.

Plymouth won 2-1 four times at Home Park.

First Goalscorers

Poole led the way for Plymouth, but the team as a whole did not score the opening goal often enough.

Team they beat twice

(Preston)
(Chester)
(Wigan)
Bournemouth

PLYMOUTH

Lost to twice last season

Exeter	Stockport
Huddersfield	Port Vale

Half-time Comparisons

Plymouth were leading in 16 matches
They were drawing in eighteen matches
And losing in twelve matches
Plymouth won 13 times when in front at the interval, and lost ten from the twelve when behind.
It was in the matches where they were level that they let themselves down badly. They won just two games from those eighteen, and lost eight.

Significant number of goals

Plymouth scored the first goal of the game just three times in their 23 away fixtures, and one of those was an own goal!
They failed to score at all in twelve of those games, and conceded two or more goals twelve times which does not give you much chance of winning.

Important games this season

Aug 28 home to Port Vale
Oct 23 away at Bristol Rovers
Dec 27 away at Exeter
Feb 5 home to Bristol Rovers
Feb 19 away at Port Vale
Apr 2 home to Exeter

Matches they need to win

At home:		Away at:	
	Huddersfield		Hull
	Hartlepool		Exeter
	Exeter		Blackpool

PORT VALE

Price performance

Vale won at their biggest price of the season when they beat West Brom at The Hawthorns. They were sent off at 5/1 at an early stage of the season when they hadn't previously won away from home. Punters would have latched on to a winning price of 5/4 if they had consulted us. Vale won five out of the six matches they played at that price, the exception being at Reading where they lost to the only goal of the game.

They also won four out of five when chalked up at 11/10.

Such results implore you to do your homework on the fixed odds coupons.

Results when odds on

Port Vale started odds on in four away games and were successful in three of them. Their only failure came at Exeter (10/11) where they drew 1-1.

They started odds on in fifteen home games and won nine of them.

Their impressive form made them 2/7 favourites to beat Mansfield which they did by three goals to nil.

It wasn't all plain sailing though, as they failed to win at 4/9, 4/7, and 8/13 twice.

Correct scores

Vale won 1-0 in five away matches, and also drew 1-1 on four occasions away from Vale Park.

They beat Mansfield, Burnley and Bournemouth 3-0, and Brighton and Reading by three goals one. They drew 2-2 three times at home.

First Goalscorers

Taylor was obviously top of the tree, but he got worthwhile support from Cross and Walker.

Teams they beat twice

(West Brom)	Huddersfield	(Chester)
Brighton	Leyton Orient	(Mansfield)
Plymouth	Blackpool	

PORT VALE

Lost to twice last season

Bradford   (Stoke)

Half-time comparisons

Port Vale were leading in 11 matches
They were drawing in 25 matches
And losing in 10 matches
Port Vale were supreme when it came to turning half time draws into winning matches. They did so 14 times during the season. They went on to win nine games when in front at the turn, and rescued three wins and three draws from those ten losing situations.

Significant number of goals

Port Vale only failed to score on three occasions away from home. These matches were at Stockport, Swansea and Reading.
They won 26 games throughout the season, and fifteen of them were by two goals or more.
Port Vale scored the first goal of the game 29 times during the season. I am still wondering how they are playing in the same division again.

Important games this season

Sep 4 home to Cardiff
Sep 25 away at Brentford
Jan 8 away at Stockport
Feb 12 home to Stockport
Feb 26 away at Cardiff
Mar 19 home to Brentford

Matches they need to win

At home: Hull
            Bradford

Away at: Rotherham
            Bournemouth
            Reading

READING

Price performance

Reading's two best away victories came at Brighton (100/30) and Leyton Orient (4/1).

They played another eleven matches at 2/1 or more with no further success.

Reading won five from seven when sent off at 11/8, but only one from five when 6/4.

They lost the only time they started at 6/5, and likewise when 5/4.

Results when odds on

Reading won six of the nine games where they started at odds on. They won at their three shortest prices of 4/9 (Chester), 4/7 (Mansfield) and 8/13 (Bournemouth). Their three failures were at 4/6, 5/6 and 10/11.

Correct scores

Reading drew 1-1 six times away from home.

They also shared four goals twice, the matches at Stockport and Plymouth coming late in the season.

Reading beat Wigan and Preston 4-0, and also won 3-0 three times at Elm Park.

They beat Rotherham and Mansfield 3-1 in front of their own supporters.

First goalscorers

Quinn led the way for Reading, ably supported by Lovell and Gilkes.

Teams they beat twice

Brighton
(Chester)

READING

Lost to twice last season
(Stoke)   (Bolton)

Half-time comparisons
Reading were leading in 11 matches
They were drawing in 22 matches
And losing in 13 matches
Reading won all eleven matches where they led at half time.
Eight of these games were at home.
They won seven and lost four of the games that were level at the
turn, and lost nine of the 13 where they were adrift.

Significant number of goals
Reading won 14 games at home, 9 of them being by two goals or
more. They only failed to score twice at home against Blackpool
and Stoke. Reading scored a maximum of one goal 18 times away
from home which proved very costly.

Important games this season
Aug 28 away Brentford
Oct 23 away at Port Vale
Oct 30 home to Fulham
Jan 29 away at Fulham
Feb 5 home to Port Vale
Feb 19 home to Brentford

Matches they need to win
At home: Hull   Away at: Hartlepool
            Blackpool   Exeter
            Exeter   Plymouth

ROTHERHAM

Price performance

Rotherham recorded good wins at Brighton (4/1) and Bradford (3/1).

They only won two games from six when priced between 5/4 and evens. Rotherham won three of the six matches where they started at 6/4.

Results when odds on

Rather surprisingly perhaps, Rotherham started sixteen matches at odds on, of which they won just six.

They only managed a draw when 1/2 to beat Chester, and won just once from four attempt when 8/13 chances.

Rotherham won two from four at both 4/6 and 8/11, and failed to win at 4/5 and 5/6.

Correct scores

Rotherham featured in two 2-2 draws away from home at West Brom and Stockport. They also shared four goals at home to Plymouth.

They drew 3-3 with Chester at Millmoor, and beat both Blackpool and Reading 3-2 at home.

Away from home, they drew 1-1 four times, and lost 0-2 four times as well.

First goalscorers

Goater and Cunningham led the way for Rotherham with Varadi chipping in as well late on in the season.

Johnson did well in away matches.

Teams they beat twice

Bradford
Brighton
(Mansfield)

ROTHERHAM

Lost to twice last season
(Stoke)

Half-time comparisons
Rotherham were leading in 11 matches
They were drawing in 24 matches
And losing in 11 matches
They did well to win ten of those eleven games where they led.
On the other side of the coin however, they lost eight of the matches where they trailed.
Rotherham both won and lost seven of the games in which they were level at the interval.

Significant number of goals
Rotherham featured in 18 games that were scoreless at half time.
They scored 21 goals in the sixteen games where they were made odds on.
Rotherham failed to score seven times at home, but only on five occasions away from Millmoor.

Important games this season
Sep 4 home to Brentford
Sep 25 away at Stockport
Oct 30 home Port Vale
Jan 29 away at Port Vale
Feb 26 away at Brentford
Mar 19 home to Stockport

Matches they need to win
At home: Hartlepool
          Hull
          Exeter
Away at: Bournemouth
          Plymouth
          Blackpool

STOCKPORT

Price performance

There were no wins for Stockport at decent prices. They started at 15/8 or more on six occasions without success.

They were bracketed between 5/4 and 7/4 most frequently, where they won 12 times from 22 attempts.

Results when odds on

Whilst Stockport won at their shortest price of the season (2/5), they failed twice at 4/9, losing one of the games to Mansfield.

They won just six times from the 16 matches where they started odds on, and they won just one game from six when priced between 4/5 and 10/11.

Stockport drew both games where they were sent off at 4/7, but they won three from four when priced as 4/6 chances.

Correct scores

Four of Stockport's five goal-less games came at home.

They drew 2-2 six times during the season. Four of these matches were at home, whilst they shared four goals at Exeter and Swansea.

Stockport lost 1-2 four times on their travels, but did win 3-2 at both Bradford and Preston.

They beat Preston, Wigan and Plymouth by three goals to nil at Edgeley Park.

First goalscorers

Francis performed brilliantly for County, particularly in front of the home supporters.

Preece, Beaumont and Gannon all gave Francis some excellent support.

Teams they beat twice

(Wigan)   (Chester)   Hull
(Preston)   Plymouth

STOCKPORT

Lost to twice last season
(Mansfield)

Half-time comparisons
Stockport were leading in 13 matches
They were drawing in 23 matches
And losing in 10 matches
Stockport won nine after being in front, and lost seven having been behind at the interval.
Where they performed well though was in the drawing situations. They turned ten of the 23 into victory, and lost just five.

Significant number of goals
County were second only to West Brom when it came to scoring goals last season.
They won nineteen games, of which 14 were by two goals or more. Indeed, seven of those victories were by a minimum of three goals.
They failed to score in twelve matches throughout the season, which makes their goal average 2.38 per game in matches where they scored at least one.

Important games this season
Nov 6 away at Cardiff
Jan 3 away at Brentford
Jan 8 home to Port Vale
Feb 12 away at Port Vale
Mar 29 home to Brentford
Apr 23 home to Cardiff

Matches they need to win

At home: Blackpool
             Bournemouth
             Rotherham

Away at: Bournemouth
             Hartlepool
             Exeter

SWANSEA

Price performance

The bookmakers got it spot on with Swansea as they won all their shortest priced games, and lost all those where they started at attractive odds.

They failed to record a victory in seven attempts when they were priced at 11/4 or more.

Swansea won two from five when classed as 6/4 chances, and won only once from six starts when priced between 6/5 and 11/8.

They won at 15/8 at Bournemouth, and 2/1 at Wigan. Those were the only times they started at such prices.

Results when odds on

Swansea started odds on seventeen times and won eleven of them.

They were a goal down at home to Wigan when starting 1/5 favourites, but came through in the second half with two goals.

Swansea only won twice in five starts when chalked up at 4/5.

Correct scores

They drew 2-2 twice at home (Stockport & Fulham) and shared six goals at Mansfield.

Swansea beat Blackpool, Hartlepool and Huddersfield by three goals to nil at home.

First goalscorers

Legg, West and Bowen all performed well for Swansea, and Harris was there for back-up as well.

Teams they beat twice

Huddersfield
Hartlepool
Bournemouth
(Wigan)
(Preston)

SWANSEA

Lost to twice last season
(Bolton)
Leyton Orient
(Stoke)

Half-time comparisons
Swansea were leading in 17 matches
They were drawing in 20 matches
And losing in 9 matches
Swansea won 12 of the games where they led, and lost six of the nine where they were behind at half time.
They won seven and lost five of the 20 games that were all square.

Significant number of goals
Swansea kept the opposition down to a maximum score of one goal in 32 of their 46 matches. They kept a clean sheet on 19 occasions (11 at home).
They lost 13 matches, eight of which were just by a single goal.
Of their twenty victories, Swansea won 12 by two goals or more.
Swansea scored two goals in a match 14 times during the season.
They won ten of these games and drew two.

Important games this season
Aug 21 home to Wrexham
Dec 11 away at Wrexham
Dec 27 away at Cardiff
Jan 1 away at Bristol Rovers
Apr 2 home to Cardiff
Apr 9 home to Bristol Rovers

Matches they need to win
At home: Exeter
              Plymouth
              Burnley

Away at: Hull
              Fulham
              Blackpool

Third Division

BURY

Price performance

Bury won all four matches when they were priced at 6/4.
Unfortunately they only won three from seven at 7/4.
Their best priced win was at 100/30 when they played at York.
They failed in all four games when sent off at 6/5, and actually
lost three of them.

Results when odds on

Their shortest prices of the season were 1/2 and 4/9, but they
failed to win either match.
Bury won two out of three at both 8/11 and 10/11.
They picked up just one point from two games when 5/6 chances.

Correct scores

Bury shared six goals at home to Northampton and beat both
Chesterfield and Doncaster 3-0 at Gigg Lane.
They won by the odd goal in five at home to Colchester and away
at Doncaster on the open day of the season.

First goalscorers

Stevens ruled the roost at Bury when scoring the opening goal
nine times. Seven of these were at home, and in those nine
games, Bury won eight of them and drew the other.

Teams they beat twice

Gillingham
Doncaster
Torquay

BURY

Lost to twice last season
Crewe

Half-time comparisons
Bury were leading in eleven games
They were drawing in 19 games
And losing in 12 games
Bury went on to win nine of the games where they led at the interval, and lost ten of the twelve where they trailed.
They won 8 and drew 4 of the 19 games that were all square.

Significant number of goals
Bury scored the opening goal of the game in twenty of the 37 games where there were goals.
They won 17 of those matches, and lost just one which was at Walsall.
Bury kept ten clean sheets at home, but only four away.

Important games this season
Aug 28 home to Crewe
Nov 20 away at Rochdale
Dec 27 away at Walsall
Feb 19 away at Crewe
Apr 2 home to Walsall
Apr 30 home to Rochdale

Matches they need to win
At home: Scarborough
             Darlington
             Lincoln

Away at: Carlisle
             Scunthorpe
             Hereford

CARLISLE

Price performance

Carlisle beat Shrewsbury when priced at 9/2, but that was their only victory in nine attempts at 100/30 or more.

They won just one match from three at both 13/5 and 3/1, Carlisle failed in all four games at 11/10, and actually lost four of them. They won once in five starts at 6/4.

Results when odds on

Carlisle only started at odds on in three matches.

They beat Gillingham at 4/5 and Northampton at 10/11, but only drew with Doncaster at 5/6.

Correct scores

Carlisle drew 2-2 in four away games and another couple at home. They shared four goals with Scarborough both at home and away.

First goalscorers

Watson and Oghani led the way for 'The Cumbrians', and Davey added useful support late on in the season.

Teams they beat twice

Shrewsbury

CARLISLE

Lost to twice last season

Walsall	(Wrexham)	Crewe
(Barnet)	Colchester	

Half-time comparisons

Carlisle were leading in 11 matches
They were drawing in 18 matches
And losing in 13 matches
They won 7 of the 11 where they led, and lost 10 of the 13 when they trailed at the turn.
Carlisle's big let down was in the matches where they were level at the interval. They won just four matches from the 18, and lost 10.

Significant number of goals

Only three teams failed to score against Carlisle when they played away from Brunton Park. These were Scunthorpe, Halifax and Torquay.
Carlisle won by a single goal just four times throughout the season, but lost eleven games the same way.
They managed to score two goals away from home on seven occasions, which helped them win three of the matches and draw the other four.

Important games this season

Oct 30 home to Walsall
Nov 20 home to Preston
Dec 28 home to Crewe
Jan 29 away at Walsall
Apr 4 away at Crewe
Apr 30 away at Preston

Matches they need to win

At home :	Scunthorpe	Away at:	Chesterfield
	Colchester		Hereford
	Torquay		Gillingham

CHESTERFIELD

Price performance

Chesterfield won three from five at 11/8, and three from six at 6/4.
They lost both their matches when priced at 5/4, but won two
from three at even money with wins over Darlington and Colchester, though they lost to Rochdale.
Chesterfield failed to win in four attempts at 7/4.

Results when odds on

Chesterfield won four from nine when priced at odds on.
They lost both their matches at 8/13 with a goal deficit of 1-6.
Chesterfield won at their shortest price of the season (4/7), but
picked up just one point from games at 4/5 and 5/6.

Correct scores

They drew 2-2 away at Torquay, Scarborough and Shrewsbury.
Chesterfield lost 1-2 five times on their travels, but won 2-1 six
times at home.
They lost 2-3 to both Rochdale and Wrexham in front of their own
supporters, and went down by the same score at Walsall.

First goalscorers

Morris and Norris (not to be confused) did well for Chesterfield,
as did Lancaster, Williams and Lemon.

Teams they beat twice

Hereford
Crewe

CHESTERFIELD

Lost to twice last season

(Barnet)   Rochdale
(Wrexham)

Half-time comparisons

Chesterfield were leading in 12 matches
They were drawing in 21 matches
And losing in 9 matches
They won 8 of the 12 matches where they led and lost 7 of the 9 when trailing at half time.
Chesterfield won seven and lost eight of the 21 matches that were level.

Significant number of goals

They only failed to score twice at home all season. These matches were against Doncaster and Scarborough.
Chesterfield only won four games by two goals or more, so their season was difficult to say the least.

Important games this season

Aug 31 home to Mansfield
Sep 18 home to Walsall
Oct 30 home to Crewe
Jan 3 away at Mansfield
Jan 29 away at Crewe
Mar 12 away at Walsall

Matches they need to win

At home: Scunthorpe
              Northampton
              Scarborough

Away at: Carlisle
              Darlington
              Doncaster

COLCHESTER

Price performance

They started at their best price of 9/2 twice, and won one of the games at Walsall.

Colchester won just a single point from three efforts at 13/8. They won once from four starts between evens and 5/4.

They won two from four at 6/4 and two of three at 11/8.

Results when odds on

Colchester started at 4/6 on four occasions. They won all four games and had a goal advantage of 8-2.

They won eight from ten at home when odds on, their only failures being at 8/11 and 5/6 when they lost both matches.

Colchester also lost at 5/6 in the only match away from home where they started odds on.

Correct scores

Colchester drew 4-4 at home to Rochdale.

They lost by the odd goal in seven at both Wrexham and Shrewesbury, and also lost 1-3 on four occasions.

Colchester beat both Walsall and Hereford three goals to one at home, They also lost 2-4 at home to both Cardiff and Wrexham.

First goalscorers

Bennett did well for Colchester, as did Abrahams at the back end of the season. He scored the only goal of the game on two occasions .

Teams they beat twice

(Halifax)	Gillingham
Walsall	Carlisle
Scarborough	

COLCHESTER

Lost to twice last season

Darlington   Shrewsbury   (Wrexham)
(Barnet)   (Cardiff)

Half-time comparisons

Colchester were leading in 16 matches
They were drawing in 12 matches
And losing in 14 matches.
Colchester lost all fourteen matches when they went in losing at half time.
They won 14 of the 16 when in front, and won four and lost four when they went in all square.

Significant number of goals

Colchester conceded seven goals at Crewe, and four goals on three occasions at Layer Road
Fifteen of Colchester's matches were decide by a single goal, and 22 were either won or lost by two goals or more.
They only failed to score eight times throughout the season.

Important games this season

Aug 21 away at Crewe
Sep 18 away at Wycombe
Oct 2 away at Preston
Dec 11 home to Crewe
Mar 12 home to Wycombe
Mar 26 home to Preston

Matches they need to win

At home: Darlington
            Shrewsbury
            Rochdale

Away at: Doncaster
            Hereford
            Northampton

CREWE

Price performance
Crewe won just once from eight efforts when priced at 2/1 or more.

They won three from nine at 6/4, and all four at prices between 6/5 and 11/8. They lost both their games at evens and 11/10.

Crewe won all three away games where they started at their shortest prices. They won at Hereford (5/4), Torquay (11/8) and Halifax (11/8).

Results when odds on
Crewe won nearly 65% of their games when they were odds on which is quite acceptable. They won 11 from 17, though they only drew with Hereford when 1/2 to win the match.

They won all seven matches in games where they were bracketed between 8/15 and 4/6, and they also won three from four when chalked up at 4/5.

Crewe did not win either game when priced up twice at 8/11, and it was a similar story at 10/11.

Correct scores
Crewe shared six goals at Scunthorpe. They also won 2-1 four times on their travels.

They beat both Doncaster and Carlisle by four goals to nil at home, and they also won 3-1 against Gillingham and York.

They were beaten 2-3 three times during the season. They lost at home to Scarborough, and away at Colchester and Barnet.

First goalscorers
Naylor, Clarkson and Edwards all performed well for their club, whilst Ward and Smith chipped in late on in the season.

Teams they beat twice
Gillingham	Carlisle	Torquay
Northampton	(Halifax)	Bury

CREWE

Lost to twice last season

Walsall   (Wrexham)
Chesterfield   Scarborough

Half-time comparisons

Crewe were leading in 18 matches
They were drawing in 12 matches
And losing in 12 matches
Crewe went on to win 16 of the 18 games where they led, and lost
ten of the twelve where they trailed.
They won five and lost three of the 12 games that were level at
the interval.

Significant number of goals

Only three teams failed to score against Crewe on their travels.
These were Rochdale, Northampton and Hereford.
They only failed to score on three occasions at home, against
Walsall, Wrexham and Chesterfield.
Crewe scored the opening goal of the game on 17 occasions at
home.

Important games this season

Aug 14 away at Preston
Aug 28 away at Bury
Sep 11 away at Walsall
Dec 18 home to Preston
Feb 19 home to Bury
Mar 5 home to Walsall

Matches they need to win

At home: Lincoln
             Chesterfield
             Scarborough

Away at: Darlington
             Walsall
             Shrewsbury

DARLINGTON

Price performance

Darlington were the team to be on when they were priced at 100/30. They won all three games at Scunthorpe, Shrewsbury and Colchester.

They started at bigger prices seven times without success.

They won just once from eight efforts when bracketed between evens and 5/4, and just once again when priced from 13/8 to 9/4.

Results when odds on

Darlington only started at odds on in four games

They picked up just one point from their three shortest priced matches. They drew at 4/5, but lost at 4/5 again and at 8/11.

Their one victory came against Northampton at odds of 5/6.

Correct scores

They drew 2-2 twice on their travels, at both Walsall and Carlisle.

They played in seven jackpot draws, with four of them coming at home.

Darlington won 3-0 at both Colchester and Scarborough.

First goalscorers

Mardenborough led the way for 'the Quakers', with Juryeff and Shaw (away from home) adding good support.

Teams they beat twice

Torquay
Colchester
Northampton

DARLINGTON

Lost to twice last season

(Halifax)   Rochdale   Lincoln

Half-time comparisons

Darlington were leading in 13 matches
They were drawing in 18 matches
And losing in 11 matches
Darlington let six matches slip, as they won just seven from their 13 winning opportunities. They lost nine of those eleven matches where they trailed.
They won four and lost five of those 18 drawing half time situations.

Significant number of goals

They failed to score in either match against Halifax last year. They were the only team to be beaten twice by 'The Shaymen' and lost by a total goal deficit of 0-4.
Darlington lost ten games at home, and five of those defeats were by two goals or more.

Important games this season

Aug 31 home to Scarborough
Sep 18 away at Crewe
Sep 25 home to Walsall
Jan 3 away at Scarborough
Mar 12 home to Crewe
Mar 19 away at Walsall

Matches they need to win

At home: Hereford   Away at: Carlisle
            Rochdale   Chesterfield
            Gillingham   Lincoln

DONCASTER

Price performance

Doncaster started at 3/1 or more (biggest price was 15/2) eleven times without success.

They won both times they were priced at 9/4 against Scunthorpe and Darlington.

Doncaster also won two from four at both 6/4 and 7/4. They lost all three games at 11/8, and lost again on the only occasion that they started at 5/4.

They only started at even money once, when they defeated Gillingham.

Results when odds on

Doncaster started at odds on on five occasion and won just once. They beat Hereford when sent off at 4/5.

They lost three of the other four matches when priced at 4/5, 8/11 and 5/6.

Correct scores

They drew 1-1 away from home on seven occasions

Doncaster lost by the only goal of the game six times in front of their own supporters.

They also lost to the odd goal in five at home to both Bury and Torquay.

First goalscorers

Jeffrey, Morrow and Gormley all contributed well for Doncaster.

Teams they beat twice

Hereford

DONCASTER

Lost to twice last season
Shrewsbury   Walsall   Bury

Half-time comparisons
Doncaster were leading in 10 matches
They were drawing in 21 matches
And losing in 11 matches
Doncaster won just fifty per cent of the games where they were
in front at the break.
They lost nine times when they trailed at half time.
Doncaster won five and lost seven of the 21 matches that were
level at the interval.

Significant number of goals
Doncaster won just one match by two goals or more. That was
when they defeated Hereford 2-0 away from home.
They lost six matches by two goals or more.
Doncaster failed to score eight times in front of their own
supporters.

Important games this season
Aug 28 away at Walsall
Nov 1 home to Scunthorpe
Jan 1 away at Crewe
Feb 19 home to Walsall
Apr 9 home to Crewe
Apr 16 Away at Scunthrope.

Matches they need to win
At home: Torquay
            Carlisle
            Darlington

Away at: Gillingham
            Shrewsbury
            Crewe

GILLINGHAM

Price performance

Gillingham started 2/1 or more (best price of 8/1) 21 times during the season, and failed to win any of them. Indeed, they lost 12 of these matches.

In contrast, they won all three games at home to Rochdale, Scarborough and Lincoln when priced 15/8.

They won just one from six when starting at either 6/5 or 5/4, but they did win on the only occasion they started at even money.

Results when odds on

Gillingham were only odds on on two occasions throughout the season.

They lost at 8/11 on the opening day of the season, but defeated Wrexham at odds of 10/11.

Correct scores

Gillingham drew 1-1 seven times away from home during the season.

They won 3-1 four times at home, but also lost 1-4 at home to both Bury and York.

Gillingham lost 1-3 three times on their travels, and also shared four goals at both Northampton and Scunthorpe.

First goalscorers

No one player stood out for Gillingham in this category. They desperately need players to open the scoring more often.

Teams they beat twice

Nil

GILLINGHAM

Lost to twice last season

Crewe   Torquay   Colchester
(Cardiff)   Bury

Half-time comparisons

Gillingham were leading in 7 matches
They were drawing in 15 matches
And losing in 20 matches
Gillingham went on to win five matches after being in front at the interval, and they lost 13 having trailed at the break.
They won four and lost six of the games that were level.

Significant number of goals

Gillingham conceded goals in every one of their 21 away matches. It is little wonder that they failed to record a victory away from the Priestfield Stadium.
They only stopped four sides from scoring against them at home.
Gillingham led at half time in five matches at home, and they won them all.

Important games this season

Sep 4 away at Wycombe
Oct 9 away at Walsall
Oct 23 away at Crewe
Jan 22 home to Walsall
Feb 5 home to Crewe
Feb 26 home to Wycombe

Matches they need to win

At home: Doncaster   Away at: Carlisle
           Northampton   Hereford
           Torquay   Darlington

HEREFORD

Price performance

Hereford had good priced victories at Rochdale (9/2)and Halifax
(100/30) and Darlington (7/2).
They were bracketed between 6/4 and 9/5 seven times without
success.
Hereford won two from three at 11/10, and likewise at 6/5 and
11/8.
They picked up just one point from three efforts at 5/4.

Results when odds on

They only started at odds on once, and that was when they lost
0-2 to Doncaster. Their odds were 4/5.

Correct scores

Hereford drew 1-1 eight times in front of their own supporters.
For good measure, they also drew 1-1 four times on their travels.
They won 3-1 four times at home, but lost 0-2 five times when
they played away from Edgar Street.
They also lost 1-3 on five occasions. Two of these defeats came at
home.

First goalscorer

Pickard led the way for Hereford, and he received fair support
from Hall, Nicholson and May.

Teams they beat twice

(Halifax)

HEREFORD

Lost to twice last season
Lincoln
Chesterfield
Doncaster

Half-time comparisons
Hereford were leading in 8 matches
They were drawing in 21 matches
And losing in 13 matches
They won five of the matches where they were leading, and lost 12 of the 13 where they were adrift at the interval.
Hereford both won and lost five times from the 21 games that were level at half time.

Significant number of goals
Hereford scored a single goal on 22 occasions so it is little wonder that they featured in so many jackpot draws.
They lost 17 matches throughout the season and thirteen of them were lost by two goals or more.
Only Halifax and Carlisle failed to score against Hereford when they played at home.

Important games this season
Aug 31 home to Wycombe
Oct 2 away at Walsall
Oct 9 away at Crewe
Jan 3 away at Wycombe
Jan 22 home to Crewe
Mar 26 home to Walsall

Matches they need to win
At home: Darlington
              Scunthorpe
              Doncaster

Away at: Gillingham
              Torquay
              Carlisle

LINCOLN

Price performance

Lincoln started at even money twice and won both games against Scarborough and Cardiff.

They won only one game from six when priced between 11/10 and 5/4.

Lincoln won fifty per cent of the fourteen matches when bracketed between 11/8 and 15/8

Good priced wins came at Crewe (11/4) and at Walsall (13/5).

Results when odds on

Lincoln failed to win at 4/9 and also at 8/15

They won three from four at 4/6, but lost all five matches between odds of 8/11 and 10/11.

Altogether Lincoln won six matches from fourteen when they started at odds on.

Correct scores

Lincoln drew 1-1 four times at home. They won 2-1 on seven occasions, with four of the victories coming away from home.

They lost 1-3 at both Gillingham and Cardiff.

First goalscorers

Costello and Baraclough featured well for Lincoln, and they received able support from Lee in particular. Matthews also helped the cause.

Teams they beat twice

Northampton
Darlington
Scarborough
Hereford

LINCOLN

Lost to twice last season

(York)   Shrewsbury
Rochdale

Half-time comparisons

Lincoln were leading in 13 matches
They were drawing in 18 matches
And losing in 11 matches
They won nine of the thirteen games when they led, and lost nine of the eleven when they found themselves trailing at the interval.
Lincoln won eight and lost four of those eighteen matches that were level.

Significant number of goals

Lincoln won ten home matches, and five of their victories were by two goals or more.
They managed to score two goals on fourteen occasions, and they won twelve of those matches and lost just one.

Important games this season

Oct 2 away at Crewe
Oct 16 away at Wycombe
Nov 20 away at Walsall
Jan 15 home to Wycombe
Mar 26 home to Crewe
Apr 30 home to Walsall

Matches they need to win

At home: Gillingham
             Torquay
             Chesterfield

Away at: Carlisle
             Gillingham
             Scunthorpe

NORTHAMPTON

Price performance

Northampton had a good record when chalked at 4/1 by the bookmakers.

They won three from six with victories at Wrexham, Chesterfield and Rochdale.

Northampton started at bigger prices on five occasions, but they lost all of them.

They did win both games at 7/2 however, and those wins came at Shrewsbury and Gillingham

Northampton won all three games when sent of 11/8, and they won two from three at 7/4.

They won just once in five starts at 6/4.

Results when odds on

Northampton secured just two draws from four matches where they started at odds on.

They lost to Halifax at 5/6, and to Torquay a 4/5. Their draws came against Gillingham (5/6) and Hereford (10/11).

Correct scores

They drew 2-2 twice on their travels. These games were at Halifax and Doncaster, whilst they shared six goals at Bury.

They won with the only goal of the game four times at home, and won by the odd goal in five at both Shrewsbury and Gillingham.

They lost 2-3 at both Crewe and Hereford, and lost 0-2 four times away from home.

First goalscorers

Brown was easily the largest contributor in this sector.

Chard set Northampton on their way to good victories at Rochdale and Chesterfield.

Teams they beat twice

Rochdale

NORTHAMPTON

Lost to twice last season

Lincoln	Darlington	Torquay
Crewe	(Cardiff)	Scarborough

Half-time comparisons

Northampton were leading in 10 matches
They were drawing in 19 matches
And losing in 13 matches
They won seven of the games when they were in front, and lost eleven of the matches where they trailed at the interval.
Northampton won just three games from the nineteen that were level. They managed to lose nine of these matches.

Significant number of goals

Only two teams failed to score against Northampton when they played away from home, the teams being Wrexham and Rochdale. Northampton won eleven games throughout the season, and eight of them were won by a single goal.

Important games this season

Aug 31 away at Crewe
Sep 4 home to Walsall
Oct 9 home to Wycombe
Jan 3 home to Crewe
Jan 22 away at Wycombe
Feb 26 away at Walsall

Matches they need to win

At home:		Away at:	
	Hereford		Hereford
	Doncaster		Torquay
	Torquay		Carlisle

ROCHDALE

Price performance

Rochdale's best priced win of the season was at Lincoln when they were returned at 100/30.

They won four from seven matches when priced at 11/8, and won both games when sent off even money and 11/10.

Rochdale only picked up one point from the games where they were priced at either 6/5 or 5/4.

They won just once from four efforts at 6/4 but won both games at 9/4 when they defeated Chesterfield (away) and York (home).

Results when odds on

Rochdale started at odds on nine times, but won just three games. Their shortest price of the season was 8/13. They failed on three occasions at that price losing all three games to a goal deficit of 3-9.

They won two from three however at 10/11, the exception being when they drew at home to Gillingham.

Correct scores

Rochdale drew 1-1 five times away from home.

They also shared eight goals at Colchester.

They won 3-2 at both Chesterfield and Halifax.

Rochdale lost 1-2 three times in front of own supporters.

First goalscorers

Flounders and Whitehall did best for Rochdale with Bowden contributing on a couple of occasions.

Teams they beat twice

Shrewsbury
Chesterfield
Torquay
Darlington
Lincoln

ROCHDALE

Lost to twice last season

(Wrexham)   Northampton
(Barnet)

Half-time comparisons

Rochdale were leading in 11 matches
They were drawing in 18 matches
And losing in 13 matches
They won ten of the games where they led, and lost nine when behind at the break.
They won four and lost seven of those 18 matches that were level at the interval.

Significant number of goals

Only two teams failed to score against Rochdale when they were away from home, and they were Torquay and Darlington.
Rochdale lost eight games away from home with seven of the defeats being by two goals or more.
Rochdale only failed to score seven times all season.

Important games this season

Oct 18 home to Walsall
Nov 6 away at Crewe
Nov 20 home to Bury
Jan 15 away at Walsall
Apr 23 home to Crewe
Apr 30 away at Bury

Matches they need to win

At home: Hereford
              Northampton
              Bury

Away at: Gillingham
              Hereford
              Carlisle

SCARBOROUGH

Price performance

Scarborough had a good win at 100/30 at Chesterfield. They also had victories when priced at 13/5 and twice at 9/4.

They started at 13/8 four times without winning, and won two from three at 11/8 and two from five at 6/4.

Scarborough won just once in four games which priced at either 6/5 or 5/4.

Results when odds on

Scarborough's record when they were made odds on was less than impressive.

They won just three games in eleven starts with victories at 8/13 and twice at 4/6.

They started between 4/5 and 10/11 seven times without success.

Correct scores

Scarborough drew 1-1 four times at home, and they shared four goals on three occasions at The Athletic Ground.

They defeated both Northampton and York by four goals to two at home, whilst they won 3-2 at both Darlington and Crewe.

Scarborough were beaten 0-3 at both Rochdale and Lincoln.

First goalscorers

Foreman and Mooney led the way at Scarborough, but the team as a whole need to score the opening goal of the game more often in front of their own supporters.

Teams they beat twice

Crewe
Torquay
Northampton
(Halifax)

SCARBOROUGH

Lost to twice last season

Lincoln   Shrewsbury
(Cardiff)   Colchester

Half-time comparisons

Scarborough were leading in 10 matches
They were drawing in 12 matches
And losing in 20 matches
They won eight of the games when in front and lost 15 of the 20
where they were behind at the turn.
Scarborough won four and lost three from those twelve drawing
situations.

Significant number of goals

Only Bury and Chesterfield failed to score against Scarborough
when they played away from home. It was not much better at
home though, as just four teams failed to find Scarborough's net.
Scarborough managed to score three goals six times on their
travels, winning five of the matches and losing 3-4 at Doncaster.

Important games this season

Aug 31 away at Darlington
Oct 16 home to Crewe
Oct 23 away at Walsall
Jan 3 home to Darlington
Jan 15 away at Crewe
Feb 5 home to Walsall

Matches they need to win

At home: Gillingham
              Doncaster
              Lincoln

Away at: Rochdale
              Shrewesbury
              Gillingham

SCUNTHORPE

Price performance

Scunthorpe failed to win in any of their six highest priced games, though they won at Scarborough at 3/1, and won twice at odds of 9/4. These games were at Carlisle and Wrexham. They also won at Chesterfield when sent off as 11/4 chances.

They won just two games from seven when priced between even money and 11/8.

Scunthorpe won both matches when priced at 7/4 to beat Doncaster (away) and Bury (home).

Results when odds on

Scunthorpe won four from nine when installed as odds on favourites.

They failed to win at their shortest price of 8/13, and won just once from three starts at 4/6.

They won their only games at 10/11 and 8/11, but won just one from three at 4/5.

Correct scores

Scunthorpe drew 2-2 twice at home and twice away.

They lost four games by the only goal of the match away from home, and were defeated 0-3 by both Barnet and Cardiff on their travels.

Scunthorpe shared six goals at home with Crewe and beat both Hereford and Colchester 3-1 at Glanford Park.

First goalscorers

Alexander and Helliwell kept Scunthorpe away from trouble on this occasion.

Teams they beat twice

Nil

SCUNTHORPE

Lost to twice last season
(York)
(Cardiff)

Half-time comparisons
Scunthorpe were leading in 15 matches
They were drawing in 16 matches
And losing in 11 matches
They won nine of those fifteen matches where they were in front
at half time, and lost nine of the eleven when they were behind.
They won five and lost five of the sixteen games that were level.

Significant number of goals
They won six matches away from home, but couldn't find the
goals to beat any of those teams at home.
Scunthorpe conceded a maximum of one goal twenty seven times
during the season which helped their cause considerably.

Important games this season
Aug 31 away at Walsall
Nov 1 away at Doncaster
Jan 3 home to Walsall
Jan 8 home to Crewe
Feb 12 away to Crewe
Apr 16 home to Doncaster

Matches they need to win

At home:	Doncaster
	Carlisle
	Torquay
Away at:	Darlington
	Hereford
	Gillingham

SHREWSBURY

Price performance

Shrewsbury won three from six when chalked up at 11/8. They won two from three at even money and two from four at 5/4. Their biggest priced wins came at Lincoln at 3/1 and at Colchester at 9/4.

Results when odds on

Shrewsbury won just five games from thirteen when they were priced up at odds on.

They failed to win from four starts when priced between 1/2 and 4/7.

Shrewsbury won both matches at 4/6, and two from three at 8/11.

Correct scores

They shared four goals twice away from home, and also drew 1-1 on four occasions when they left Gay Meadow.

They defeated both Cardiff and Lincoln by three goals to two at home, whilst they lost by the same score at home to both Carlisle and Northampton.

First goalscorers

Griffiths was by far and away Shrewsbury's hero in the goalscoring department. He scored well over fifty per cent of all their opening goals during the season. His performances alone nearly took Shrewsbury to a play-off place.

Teams they beat twice

Colchester
Lincoln
Scarborough
Doncaster

SHREWSBURY

Lost to twice last season

Rochdale	(Wrexham)
Carlisle	Torquay

Half-time comparisons

Shrewsbury were leading in 14 matches
They were drawing in 14 matches
And losing in 14 matches
They did well to win 12 of those 14 games where they led, but lost eight of the matches where they were behind.
Shrewsbury won just three and lost five of those fourteen drawing situations.

Significant number of goals

Twenty one of Shrewsbury's matches were decided by a single goal.
They scored just eight goals in the first half in their collective away games. Fortunately they scored another thirteen after the break.

Important games this season

Aug 21 home to Walsall
Oct 30 away at Wycombe
Nov 2 home to Crewe
Dec 11 away at Walsall
Jan 29 home to Wycombe
Apr 16 away at Crewe

Matches they need to win

At home:	Rochdale
	Walsall
	Carlisle
Away at:	Northampton
	Torquay
	Hereford

TORQUAY

Price performance

Torquay won at Shrewsbury at odds of 4/1, but that was their only victory in twelve efforts at odds of 11/4 or more.

They won two from five at 13/8 and failed to win in four attempts at 15/8.

Torquay picked up just a point from two games at 5/4, and they won just two from five when priced at either 11/10 or 6/5.

Results at odds on

Torquay started just three matches at odds on.

They won just the one, that game being against Northampton when they were sent of as 4/5 chances.

Torquay drew at 4/5 and lost at home to Carlisle at 5/6.

Correct Scores

Torquay shared four goals on five occasions throughout the season.

They drew 2-2 with both Chesterfield and Colchester at home, whilst they forced a high scoring draw at Lincoln, Scunthorpe and Walsall.

Torquay lost to the only goal of the game four times at home.

First goalscorers

Several players put in a claim to be Torquay's goalscoring saviour, but none really stood out

Darby, Kelly, Joyce and Foster all played their part in keeping Torquay afloat.

Teams they beat twice

Northampton
Shrewsbury
(Halifax)
Gillingham

TORQUAY

Lost to twice last season

Rochdale	Scarborough	Bury
Crewe	Darlington	(Barnet)

Half time comparisons

Torquay were leading in 8 matches
They were drawing in 15 matches
And losing in 19 matches
Torquay won five of those games when they were in front and lost fourteen of the nineteen matches where they were behind.
They won five and lost seven of those fifteen games that were level.

Significant number of goals

Torquay won twelve matches during the course of the season, and nine of those victories were won by a single goal.

Important games this season

Sep 18 home to Preston
Sep 25 home to Crewe
Dec 27 home to Wycombe
Mar 12 away at Preston
Mar 19 away at Crewe
Apr 2 away at Wycombe

Matches they need to win

At home:	Carlisle
	Doncaster
	Darlington
Away at:	Hereford
	Colchester
	Chesterfield

WALSALL

Price Performance
Walsall won all three matches when priced at even money.
They won two from three at 6/5 and three from six at 6/4.
Walsall won at their biggest price of the season which was
100/30. They beat York 1-0 away from home.

Results when odds on
Walsall had a fifty per cent success record at odds on. They won
eight games with their shortest price (2/7) coming at home to
Rochdale who they defeated 3-1.
They played seven games between the odds of 4/7 and 8/11 and
failed to win any of them.

Correct Scores
Walsall drew 1-1 in four of their home matches.
They also shared four goals at home to both Darlington and
Torquay.
Walsall won 3-1 three times in front of their own supporters, and
they beat Scarborough, Scunthorpe and Chesterfield by three
goals to two.
They won 1-0 four times on their travels, and won by the odd goal
in seven at home to Bury. They also won 4-3 at Carlisle.

First goalscorers
Cecere and Clarke did well for Walsall, and MacDonald was
particularly effective away from home.

Teams they beat twice
(York)
Doncaster
Carlisle
Crewe

WALSALL

Lost to twice last season
(Cardiff)   Colchester

Half time comparisons
Walsall were leading in 17 matches
They were drawing in 13 matches
And losing in 12 matches
Walsall went on to win 15 of the 17 matches where they led at the interval, and lost 9 of the 12 where they trailed.
They won six and lost three of the thirteen matches that were level at the break.

Significant number of goals
Walsall scored in every home game of the season. They also failed to score on just three occasions away from home.
They scored forty two goals at home with thirty of those coming in the second half.

Important games this season
Sep 11 home to Crewe
Dec 27 home to Bury
Jan 1 home to Wycombe
Mar 5 away at Crewe
Apr 2 away at Bury
Apr 9 away at Wycombe

Matches they need to win
At home: Darlington
            Lincoln
            Gillingham

Away at: Northampton
            Rochdale
            Scunthorpe

Scottish League Football

We have changed the format in our team by team guide, as Scottish clubs play each other so frequently.

On the following pages however, you will still find any correct scores that became repetitive involving the club in question. Once again you will find that the correct scores quoted would have given you a profit to level stake betting last year.

The majority of information you will find concentrates on the number of points each club took from each other during the course of the season.

The number of points are listed against each club, alongside the actual results of the games, together with the price that the team concerned started at. These are listed separately for home and away purposes.

Scottish Premier Division

ABERDEEN

		Home		Away	
Hibernian	8 pts	Won 8/11	Won 4/7	Won 6/4	Won 11/10
Partick	8 pts	Won 4/7	Won 4/11	Won 6/5	Won 10/11
Dundee	7 pts	Won 4/7	Drew 2/5	Won 2/1	Won 10/11
St. Johnstone	7 pts	Won 2/5	Drew 2/5	Won 5/4	Won 5/6
Motherwell	6 pts	Won 1/3	Won 1/3	Lost 11/10	Won 5/6
Hearts	6 pts	Won 11/10	Won 8/11	Lost 7/4	Won 6/4
Dundee Utd.	4 pts	Lost 4/5	Drew 8/13	Drew 6/4	Won 6/4
Celtic	3 pts	Drew 6/4	Drew 4/5	Drew 7/4	Lost 13/8
Rangers	2 pts	Lost 13/8	Won 13/8	Lost 4/1	Lost 10/3

Correct Scores

Aberdeen won five matches away by two goals to one.

They also shared four goals at both Dundee United and Celtic.

CELTIC

		Home		Away	
Dundee	8 pts	Won 8/11	Won 2/5	Won 5/4	Won 5/4
St. Johnstone	6 pts	Won 4/11	Won 8/13	Draw 4/6	Draw 11/10
Dundee Utd.	5 pts	Won 8/11	Lost 8/11	Draw 7/4	Won 11/8
Partick	5 pts	Lost 4/11	Drew 8/15	Won 4/5	Won 11/10
Hearts	5 pts	Drew 4/5	Won 10/11	Won 8/5	Lost 13/8
Aberdeen	5 pts	Drew 5/4	Won 5/4	Drew 6/4	Drew 3/1
Motherwell	4 pts	Drew 2/5	Drew 8/13	Won 1/1	Lost 4/5
Hibernian	4 pts	Lost 8/15	Won 4/7	Won 5/4	Lost 6/5
Rangers	3 pts	Lost 7/4	Won 15/8	Drew 15/8	Lost 10/3

Correct Scores

Celtic won nine games in all by one goal to nil, five of those victories coming away from home.

They also won by the odd goal in five three times. They beat Falkirk at home, and both Partick and Dundee United away.

Celtic also played in six 1-1 matches away from Celtic Park, which included two jackpot draws at Aberdeen.

DUNDEE

		Home		Away	
Motherwell	7 pts	Won 11/8	Drew 11/10	Won 13/8	Won 5/2
Hibernian	6 pts	Drew 5/4	Won 8/13	Drew 10/3	Won 9/4
St. Johnstone	5 pts	Drew 11/8	Won 5/4	Drew 13/5	Drew 13/8
Hearts	3 pts	Lost 2/1	Won 2/1	Lost 9/2	Drew 5/1
Rangers	2 pts	Won 7/1	Lost 6/1	Lost 12/1	Lost 9/1
Dundee Utd.	2 pts	Lost 15/8	Lost 13/8	Won 7/2	Lost 13/5
Aberdeen	1 pt	Lost 9/4	Lost 13/5	Lost 9/2	Drew 7/1
Celtic	- pts	Lost 7/4	Lost 7/4	Lost 11/2	Lost 13/2
Partick	- pts	Lost 11/10	Lost 6/5	Lost 7/4	Lost 6/4

Correct Scores

Dundee lost seven matches by one goal to nil with four of them coming away from home.

They lost 1-3 on their own patch to three teams, they were Rangers, Hearts and Dundee United. For the record, Rangers also beat them 3-1 in one of their games at Ibrox.

DUNDEE UNITED

		Home		Away	
Partick	8 pts	Won 8/13	Won 8/15	Won 11/10	Won 6/4
Dundee	6 pts	Lost 4/6	Won 10/11	Won 11/8	Won 5/4
St. Johnstone	4 pts	Won 4/6	Lost 4/7	Lost 6/5	Won 11/8
Motherwell	4 pts	Drew 4/7	Drew 8/13	Won 8/5	Lost 11/8
Aberdeen	4 pts	Drew 13/8	Lost 6/4	Won 3/1	Drew 9/2
Celtic	3 pts	Drew 6/4	Lost 9/5	Lost 7/2	Won 10/3
Hibernian	2 pts	Won 5/6	Lost 8/15	Lost 6/4	Lost 9/5
Hearts	1 pt	Drew 6/5	Lost 5/4	Lost 9/4	Lost 13/5
Rangers	1 pt	Lost 9/4	Drew 9/4	Lost 6/1	Lost 4/1

Correct Scores

Dundee United won by one goal to nil four times away from
home. They also won 4-0 at both Partick and Dundee.

HEARTS

		Home		Away	
Dundee United	7 pts	Won 1/1	Won 10/11	Drew 2/1	Won 2/1
Hibernian	6 pts	Won 4/5	Won 4/5	Drew 8/5	Drew 6/4
Partick	5 pts	Won 1/2	Drew 8/15	Drew 5/4	Drew 5/4
Motherwell	5 pts	Won 8/15	Drew 1/2	Won 11/10	Lost 11/8
Dundee	5 pts	Won 4/7	Drew 8/15	Lost 11/10	Won 5/4
St. Johnstone	4 pts	Drew 8/15	Won 8/13	Drew 6/4	Lost 7/4
Celtic	3 pts	Lost 8/5	Won 13/8	Drew 7/2	Lost 13/5
Aberdeen	2 pts	Won 5/4	Lost 11/8	Lost 10/3	Lost 9/4
Rangers	1 pt	Drew 9/4	Lost 2/1	Lost 9/2	Lost 11/2

Correct Scores

Hearts won eight matches by one goal to nil in front of their own supporters.

They also drew 1-1 nine times during the season, with five of the games coming away from home.

HIBERNIAN

		Home		Away	
		Home		Away	
Motherwell	6 pts	Drew 4/6	Won 5/4	Won 6/4	Drew 7/4
Dundee Utd.	6 pts	Won 6/4	Won 11/8	Lost 13/5	Won 9/2
Partick	5 pts	Lost 6/5	Won 10/11	Drew 6/4	Won 6/4
St. Johnstone	4 pts	Drew 10/11	Won 8/11	Drew 13/8	Lost 9/5
Celtic	4 pts	Lost 2/1	Won 15/8	Won 5/1	Lost 5/1
Hearts	2 pts	Drew 8/5	Drew 7/4	Lost 7/2	Lost 3/1
Dundee	2 pts	Drew 8/11	Lost 1/1	Drew 7/4	Lost 3/1
Rangers	1 pt	Drew 7/2	Lost 9/2	Lost 15/2	Lost 9/1
Aberdeen	0 pts	Lost 6/4	Lost 2/1	Lost 7/2	Lost 9/2

Correct Scores

Hibernian won four games at home by three goals to one. Their victims were Celtic, Falkirk, St. Johnstone and Airdrie.

MOTHERWELL

		Home		Away	
Dundee Utd.	4 pts	Lost 8/5	Won 9/5	Drew 5/1	Drew 4/1
Celtic	4 pts	Lost 9/4	Won 3/1	Drew 7/1	Drew 9/2
St. Johnstone	3 pts	Drew 6/5	Drew 1/1	Lost 10/3	Drew 7/4
Hearts	3 pts	Lost 2/1	Won 6/4	Lost 5/1	Drew 11/2
Partick	3 pts	Lost 11/8	Lost 4/5	Drew 7/4	Won 13/5
Hibernian	2 pts	Lost 6/4	Drew 5/4	Drew 4/1	Lost 13/8
Aberdeen	2 pts	Won 11/5	Lost 11/4	Lost 8/1	Lost 13/2
Dundee	1 pt	Lost 11/8	Lost 10/11	Lost 13/8	Drew 2/1
Rangers	0 pts	Lost 9/2	Lost 5/1	Lost 10/1	Lost 8/1

Correct Scores

Motherwell lost 0-1 in five away games. They also lost 1-3 at home to Celtic, Dundee and Hearts.

They drew 1-1 four times on their travels, with two of the results occurring at Celtic Park.

PARTICK

		Home		Away	
Dundee	8 pts	Won 11/8	Won 6/4	Won 2/1	Won 15/8
Motherwell	5 pts	Drew 6/4	Lost 5/6	Won 9/5	Won 3/1
St. Johnstone	5 pts	Won 11/10	Drew 5/4	Drew 5/2	Drew 10/3
Hibernian	3 pts	Drew 6/4	Lost 6/4	Lost 13/5	Won 13/5
Hearts	3 pts	Drew 2/1	Drew 7/4	Lost 6/1	Drew 11/2
Celtic	3 pts	Lost 3/1	Lost 15/8	Won 13/2	Drew 11/2
Rangers	2 pts	Lost 5/1	Won 3/1	Lost 11/1	Lost 9/1
Dundee Utd.	0 pts	Lost 12/5	Lost 6/4	Lost 4/1	Lost 10/3
Aberdeen	0 pts	Lost 15/8	Lost 9/4	Lost 9/2	Lost 15/2

Correct Scores

Partick did not figure particularly in any repetitive scorelines.

RANGERS

		Home		Away	
Motherwell	8 pts	Won 1/4	Won 2/7	Won 4/7	Won 4/9
St. Johnstone	7 pts	Won 1/3	Won 1/3	Won 2/5	Drew 4/9
Hearts	7 pts	Won 4/7	Won 8/15	Drew 6/5	Won 11/10
Hibernian	7 pts	Won 4/11	Won 4/11	Drew 8/11	Won 4/6
Dundee Utd.	7 pts	Won 4/9	Won 1/2	Won 1/1	Drew 11/10
Aberdeen	6 pts	Won 8/11	Won 8/11	Won 13/8	Lost 6/4
Dundee	6 pts	Won 1/5	Won 2/9	Lost 4/9	Won 4/9
Partick	6 pts	Won 2/7	Won 2/7	Won 8/15	Lost 8/13
Celtic	5 pts	Drew 5/4	Won 8/11	Won 8/11	Lost 6/4

Correct Scores

Rangers won by one goal to nil on five occasions at home. For good measure they also won by the same scoreline three times on their travels.

They won 4-0 at both Dundee United and Motherwell, and won 4-1 at Motherwell again, and at Partick.

ST JOHNSTONE

		Home		Away	
Motherwell	5 pts	Won 8/11	Drew 6/5	Drew 7/4	Drew 9/2
Hibernian	4 pts	Drew 11/8	Won 5/4	Lost 10/3	Drew 5/2
Dundee Utd.	4 pts	Won 9/4	Lost 13/8	Lost 4/1	Won 5/1
Hearts	4 pts	Drew 13/8	Won 5/4	Drew 11/2	Lost 9/2
Partick	3 pts	Drew 10/11	Won 8/11	Lost 2/1	Drew 7/4
Dundee	3 pts	Drew 10/11	Drew 5/4	Drew 15/8	Lost 7/4
Celtic	2 pts	Drew 4/1	Drew 2/1	Lost 13/2	Lost 7/2
Aberdeen	1 pt	Lost 7/4	Lost 11/4	Lost 7/1	Drew 11/2
Rangers	1 pt	Lost 7/1	Drew 6/1	Lost 10/1	Lost 12/1

Correct Scores

As the tables in this book indicate, St. Johnstone were the draw kings of the Premier Division.

They took part in twelve 1-1 draws, with an even split of six each home and away.

St. Johnstone also split eight goals with Dundee United on one occasion.

They drew 2-2 at Falkirk in the two matches they played at Brockville Park, and also shared four goals at Hibernian. For good measure they drew 3-3 at Motherwell.

Scottish First Division

AYR UNITED

		Home		Away	
Dunfermline	6 pts	Drew 6/4	Won 11/8	Won 4/1	Drew 4/1
Hamilton	6 pts	Drew 11/8	Won 7/4	Drew 3/1	Won 4/1
Stirling	5 pts	Won 10/11	Drew 4/6	Drew 5/4	Drew 11/8
Clydebank	5 pts	Won 11/10	Drew 10/11	Drew 2/1	Drew 5/2
Dumbarton	5 pts	Won 5/4	Drew 1/1	Won 2/1	Lost 7/4
St. Mirren	3 pts	Won 11/8	Drew 11/4	Lost 7/2	Lost 7/2
Morton	1 pt	Lost 5/4	Drew 5/4	Lost 5/2	Lost 5/2

Correct Scores
Ayr featured in seven away matches that ended 1-1.

CLYDEBANK

		Home		Away	
Stirling	7 pts	Won 5/6	Drew 8/11	Won 11/8	Won 5/2
Dunfermline	5 pts	Won 11/8	Drew 7/4	Won 4/1	Lost 10/3
Dumbarton	4 pts	Lost 10/11	Won 10/11	Lost 7/4	Won 7/4
Ayr	3 pts	Drew 11/10	Drew 5/6	Lost 9/5	Drew 12/5
Hamilton	2 pts	Won 5/4	Lost 13/8	Lost 3/1	Lost 5/2
Morton	2 pts	Drew 6/5	Drew 5/4	Lost 11/5	Lost 5/2
St. Mirren	1 pt	Lost 11/8	Lost 5/4	Drew 4/1	Lost 11/5

Correct Scores

Clydebank drew five of their home matches 1-1.

They beat Raith, Cowdenbeath and Stirling by four goals to one at Kilbowie Park. They also won 3-1 on three occasions at home. They beat Hamilton, Dumbarton and Meadowbank.

Clydebank also played in two 3-3 draws away from home. These matches were at Cowdenbeath and Kilmarnock.

DUMBARTON

		Home		Away	
Stirling	4 pts	Won 1/1	Lost 4/5	Won 6/4	Lost 11/8
Morton	4 pts	Lost 6/4	Won 6/4	Won 10/3	Lost 5/2
St. Mirren	4 pts	Won 9/5	Won 11/8	Lost 11/4	Lost 10/3
Clydebank	4 pts	Won 6/5	Lost 6/5	Won 9/4	Lost 12/5
Hamilton	4 pts	Drew 6/4	Won 11/8	Lost 5/2	Drew 7/2
Ayr	3 pts	Lost 1/1	Won 6/5	Lost 13/8	Drew 2/1
Dunfermline	2 pts	Lost 6/4	Drew 7/2	Lost 4/1	Drew 9/2

Correct Scores:-

Dumbarton lost 2-3 at both Hamilton and Dunfermline.

Dumbarton beat Stirling 4-3 at home, but lost 3-5 at Ayr. Goals were usually on the agenda when Dumbarton played.

DUNFERMLINE

		Home		Away	
Hamilton	6 pts	Won 5/6	Won 5/4	Lost 6/4	Won 11/8
Dumbarton	6 pts	Won 4/7	Drew 8/15	Won 11/8	Drew 1/2
Stirling	6 pts	Won 8/15	Lost 4/9	Won 5/4	Won 5/6
Morton	5 pts	Drew 1/1	Lost 1/3	Won 11/8	Won 6/4
St. Mirren	4 pts	Won 11/8	Lost 8/13	Lost 7/4	Won 6/4
Clydebank	3 pts	Lost 4/7	Won 4/6	Lost 6/4	Drew 11/10
Ayr	2 pts	Lost 4/7	Drew 4/7	Lost 6/4	Drew 11/8

Correct Scores

Dunfermline won 1-0 six times away from home.

They beat Dumbarton and Meadowbank by three goals to two at East End Park, and also won by the same scoreline at Kilmarnock.

Dunfermline shared four goals at home with both Dumbarton and Kilmarnock.

HAMILTON

		Home		Away	
Stirling	7 pts	Won 4/7	Won 8/13	Won 11/8	Drew 10/11
Motherwell	6 pts	Won 6/5	Won 10/11	Lost 9/4	Won 13/8
Clydebank	6 pts	Won 8/13	Won 4/5	Lost 6/4	Won 5/4
St. Mirren	4 pts	Drew 6/5	Drew 6/5	Won 2/1	Lost 5/2
Dumbarton	4 pts	Won 4/5	Drew 8/13	Drew 11/8	Lost 11/8
Ayr	2 pts	Drew 8/11	Lost 4/7	Drew 6/4	Lost 6/5
Dunfermline	2 pts	Won 11/8	Lost 6/4	Lost 5/2	Lost 13/8

Correct Scores

Hamilton beat both Meadowbank and Cowdenbeath 4-0 away from home.

They also lost 1-2 five times on their travels, which included both the games at Dunfermline.

Hamilton lost two matches at home by three goals to one.

MORTON

		Home		Away	
Ayr	7 pts	Won 5/6	Won 5/6	Won 6/4	Drew 13/8
Clydebank	6 pts	Won 1/1	Won 5/6	Drew 7/4	Drew 13/8
Dumbarton	4 pts	Lost 4/6	Won 4/5	Won 11/8	Lost 11/8
Stirling	4 pts	Drew 1/2	Lost 11/10	Drew 11/10	Won 1/1
St. Mirren	3 pts	Lost 5/4	Drew 11/8	Won 11/4	Lost 2/1
Dunfermline	3 pts	Lost 6/4	Lost 8/11	Drew 11/5	Won 11/2
Hamilton	2 pts	Won 10/11	Lost 5/4	Lost 7/4	Lost 9/4

Correct Scores

Morton drew 2-2 away on three occasions. Two of them came at Clydebank and the other at Kilmarnock.

STIRLING

		Home		Away	
Morton	4 pts	Drew 7/4	Lost 2/1	Drew 5/1	Won 13/8
Dumbarton	4 pts	Lost 11/8	Won 6/4	Lost 2/1	Won 5/2
St. Mirren	3 pts	Lost 9/4	Won 7/4	Drew 4/1	Lost 7/2
Ayr	3 pts	Drew 13/8	Drew 11/8	Drew 10/3	Lost 9/4
Dunfermline	2 pts	Lost 6/4	Lost 11/4	Lost 5/1	Won 6/1
Hamilton	1 pt	Lost 11/8	Drew 12/5	Lost 4/1	Lost 7/2
Clydebank	1 pt	Lost 6/4	Lost 4/5	Lost 5/2	Drew 3/1

Correct Scores

Stirling won four of their home games 2-1.

They drew 1-1 four times on their travels, and also shared four goals at both Ayr and Morton.

ST MIRREN

		Home		Away	
Clydebank	7 pts	Drew 4/7	Won 1/1	Won 6/4	Won 13/8
Stirling	5 pts	Drew 4/7	Won 8/13	Won 10/11	Lost 6/5
Ayr	5 pts	Won 8/13	Won 8/13	Lost 6/4	Drew 4/6
Morton	5 pts	Lost 5/6	Won 1/1	Won 13/8	Drew 6/4
Dumbarton	4 pts	Won 4/5	Won 4/6	Lost 11/10	Lost 6/4
Dunfermline	4 pts	Won 6/5	Lost 11/8	Lost 6/4	Won 7/2
Hamilton	4 pts	Lost 11/10	Won 4/5	Drew 7/4	Drew 7/4

Correct Scores

St. Mirren won five away games by two goals to one. They also won four games by the same margin at home.

They shared six goals at Ayr.

Scottish Second Division

ALBION ROVERS

		Home		Away	
Queen O.T. Sth	4 pts	Won 6/4	Lost 6/4	Won 9/4	–
East Stirling	4 pts	Drew 11/10	–	Drew 15/8	Won 5/2
Queen's Park	3 pts	Won 5/4	–	Lost 2/1	Drew 5/2
Berwick	2 pts	Drew 11/10	–	Lost 6/4	Drew 5/2
Montrose	2 pts	Drew 6/5	–	Lost 5/2	Drew 5/2
Forfar	2 pts	Won 5/2	–	Lost 5/1	Lost 6/1
East Fife	2 pts	Lost 5/4	Won 12/5	Lost 4/1	–
Stranraer	2 pts	Drew 2/1	Lost 2/1	Drew 7/2	–
Stenhousemuir	1 pt	Drew 7/4	Lost 7/4	Lost 13/8	–
Alloa	0 pts	Lost 6/4	–	Lost 4/1	Lost 6/1
Arbroath	0 pts	Lost 13/8	Lost 9/4	Lost 7/4	–

Correct Scores

Albion lost 0-2 in five away games last season. They also drew 1-1 in five further matches away from Clifton Hill Stadium.

ALLOA

		Home		Away	
Albion	6 pts	Won 4/7	Won 4/9	Won 11/8	–
Montrose	6 pts	Won 4/6	Won 4/7	Won 5/2	–
Queen O.S.	5 pts	Drew 11/8	–	Won 2/1	Won 11/8
Stenhousr	4 pts	Won 8/13	Lost 5/6	Won 2/1	–
Queen's Park	4 pts	Drew 8/13	–	Won 7/4	Drew 5/4
E. Stirling	4 pts	Won 8/11	–	Lost 11/8	Won 6/5
Berwick	3 pts	Won 8/13	Lost 4/7	Drew 5/4	–
Stranraer	3 pts	Lost 11/10	–	Won 2/1	Drew 10/3
Forfar	3 pts	Drew 6/5	–	Drew 5/2	Drew 5/2
Arbroath	1 pt	Lost 8/11	Lost 4/5	Drew 7/4	–
East Fife	1 pt	Lost 4/5	–	Lost 7/4	Drew 13/8

Correct Scores

Alloa lost 0-2 at home on four occasions.

They shared four goals three times at East Fife, Berwick and Queen's Park.

They also drew 2-2 at home against Queen of the South.

ARBROATH

		Home		Away	
Albion	6 pts	Won 6/5	Won 5/4	Won 10/11	–
Stenhousemuir	6 pts	Won 1/1	Won 5/6	Won 2/1	–
Queen O.T.S.	5 pts	Drew 5/4	–	Won 2/1	Won 5/4
Alloa	5 pts	Drew 6/5	–	Won 3/1	Won 5/2
Queen's Park	4 pts	Won 4/5	–	Won 6/4	Lost 6/5
East Fife	4 pts	Lost 5/4	Won 5/6	Won 5/2	–
East Stirling	3 pts	Lost 8/11	Drew 4/7	Won 6/5	–
Forfar	2 pts	Lost 5/4	Drew 11/10	Drew 7/2	–
Stranraer	2 pts	Won 6/4	Lost 7/4	Lost 10/3	–
Berwick	2 pts	Lost 8/11	Won 10/11	Lost 2/1	–
Montrose	1 pt	Lost 11/8	–	Drew 13/8	Lost 5/6

Correct Scores

Arbroath played in five 0-0 draws in front of their own supporters. However, goals could be found at Gayfield Park as Arbroath
triumphed over Berwick 6-0, but lost 3-4 to Montrose and 4-5 to
East Stirling.

BERWICK

		Home		Away	
Montrose	6 pts	Won 6/4	Won 8/13	Won 4/1	–
Arbroath	4 pts	Won 1/1	–	Won 3/1	Lost 12/5
Albion	4 pts	Drew 4/5	Drew 7/4	Won 11/8	–
Stenhousemuir	4 pts	Drew 6/4	–	Won 11/5	Drew 12/5
East Fife	4 pts	Won 6/4	Lost 7/2	Won 2/1	–
Forfar	4 pts	Won 2/1	–	Lost 10/3	Won 4/1
Queen's Park	3 pts	Won 4/6	Drew 4/6	Lost 11/8	–
Alloa	3 pts	Drew 13/8	–	Lost 7/2	Won 4/1
Stranraer	2 pts	Lost 6/4	–	Won 5/1	Lost 8/1
Queen O.T.S.	2 pts	Lost 1/1	Won 4/5	Lost 15/8	–
East Stirling	1 pt	Lost 8/11	Drew 4/7	Lost 6/4	–

Correct Scores

Berwick beat East Fife, Queen of the South and Montrose by three goals to nil at home.

They also beat Stranraer, Montrose and Stenhousemuir by three goals to one on their travels.

EAST FIFE

		Home		Away	
Alloa	5 pts	Won 6/5	Drew 6/4	Won 5/2	–
East Stirling	5 pts	Drew 4/7	–	Won 11/8	Won 11/10
Queen's Park	5 pts	Won 8/13	–	Won 5/4	Drew 5/4
Albion	4 pts	Won 4/7	–	Won 13/8	Lost 10/11
Stenhousemuir	3 pts	Won 1/1	Drew 8/13	Lost 15/8	–
Forfar	3 pts	Lost 1/1	–	Drew 11/4	Won 5/2
Montrose	3 pts	Lost 6/5	Drew 8/13	Won 13/8	–
Berwick	2 pts	Won 4/6	Lost 1/1	Lost 11/8	–
Arbroath	2 pts	Lost 4/5	–	Won 6/4	Lost 12/5
Queen O.T.S.	1 pt	Lost 4/5	–	Drew 13/8	Lost 11/8
Stranraer	1 pt	Lost 11/8	Drew 11/8	Lost 13/8	–

Correct Scores

East Fife won 3-1 four times away from home. They also shared four goals at Clyde, Forfar and Queen's Park.

They lost 2-3 at home to both Montrose and Clyde. There were also two 2-2 draws at Bayview Park against East Stirling and Alloa.

EAST STIRLING

		Home		Away	
Berwick	5 pts	Won 11/8	–	Won 3/1	Drew 4/1
Arbroath	3 pts	Lost 7/4	–	Won 3/1	Drew 4/1
Queen's Park	3 pts	Drew 6/5	Won 11/8	Lost 11/8	–
Queen O.T.S.	2 pts	Lost 4/5	Lost 6/4	Won 5/2	–
Alloa	2 pts	Won 6/4	Lost 7/4	Lost 3/1	–
Albion	2 pts	Drew 11/10	Lost 5/6	Drew 7/4	–
Stenhousemuir	2 pts	Lost 11/10	–	Won 3/1	Lost 7/2
Forfar	2 pts	Won 15/8	Lost 2/1	Lost 4/1	–
Montrose	1 pt	Lost 7/4	Drew 11/10	Lost 5/2	–
Stranraer	1 pt	Lost 6/4	–	Lost 7/2	Drew 4/1
East Fife	1 pt	Lost 6/4	Lost 2/1	Drew 4/1	–

Correct Scores

East Stirling lost five home matches by two goals to one, including two against Queen of the South.

Away from Firs Park, they lost 1-4 to both Stranraer and Montrose, and 1-5 at Clyde and Forfar.

East Stirling drew 2-2 at both Albion and East Fife.

FORFAR

		Home		Away	
Montrose	5 pts	Won 8/15	–	Drew 6/4	Won 3/1
Queen O.T.S.	5 pts	Won 8/13	–	Drew 11/8	Won 5/4
Queen's Park	5 pts	Won 8/15	Drew 4/9	Won 6/5	–
Arbroath	4 pts	Drew 4/6	–	Won 13/8	Drew 7/4
Stenhousemuir	4 pts	Won 4/7	Won 4/6	Lost 13/8	–
East Stirling	4 pts	Won 4/7	–	Lost 11/10	Won 1/1
Albion	4 pts	Won 1/2	Won 4/9	Lost 5/6	–
Alloa	3 pts	Drew 4/5	Drew 4/5	Drew 7/4	–
East Fife	3 pts	Drew 5/6	Lost 5/6	Won 2/1	–
Stranraer	2 pts	Won 4/5	–	Lost 11/5	Lost 2/1
Berwick	2 pts	Won 4/6	Lost 4/7	Lost 11/10	–

Correct Scores

Forfar beat Queen of the South and East Stirling by five goals to one at home. During the course of the season, they also won 5-2 and 5-3 at Station Park.

MONTROSE

		Home		Away	
East Stirling	5 pts	Won 4/5	–	Won 6/5	Drew 7/4
Arbroath	5 pts	Drew 5/4	Won 5/2	Won 11/8	–
Queen O.T.S.	4 pts	Won 5/6	Lost 11/8	Won 13/8	–
Albion	4 pts	Won 4/5	Drew 4/5	Drew 7/4	–
East Fife	3 pts	Lost 5/4	–	Won 7/4	Drew 7/2
Queen's Park	2 pts	Lost 2/5	Won 5/4	Lost 6/4	–
Forfar	1 pt	Drew 11/8	Lost 5/2	Lost 10/3	–
Stranraer	0 pts	Lost 8/11	Lost 4/1	Lost 10/3	–
Stenhousemuir	0 pts	Lost 8/13	Lost 11/8	Lost 6/4	–
Alloa	0 pts	Lost 4/5	–	Lost 10/3	Lost 4/1
Berwick	0 pts	Lost 4/7	–	Lost 7/2	Lost 10/3

Correct Scores

Montrose lost 1-3 on four occasions away from home. They also lost by the same scoreline three times at Links Park.

Alloa and Stenhousemuir both beat Montrose 4-1 at Montrose.

QUEEN OF THE SOUTH

		Home		Away	
Queen's Park	5 pts	Won 5/6	–	Won 11/8	Drew 11/8
East Fife	5 pts	Drew 5/4	Won 11/8	Won 5/2	–
East Stirling	4 pts	Lost 4/5	–	Won 5/2	Won 11/8
Stranraer	4 pts	Won 7/4	Drew 15/8	Drew 9/4	–
Berwick	4 pts	Won 11/10	–	Won 2/1	Lost 12/5
Albion	2 pts	Lost 10/11	–	Lost 11/8	Won 11/8
Montrose	2 pts	Lost 5/4	–	Lost 5/2	Won 6/4
Alloa	1 pt	Lost 1/1	Lost 11/8	Drew 3/1	–
Stenhousemuir	1 pt	Lost 4/5	–	Drew 10/3	Lost 11/4
Forfar	1 pt	Drew 6/4	Lost 13/8	Lost 7/2	–
Arbroath	1 pt	Lost 11/10	Lost 13/8	Drew 13/8	–

Correct Scores

Queen of the South drew 2-2 at both Stranraer and Alloa.

They shared six goals with Stranraer in front of their home supporters.

They also lost 1-2 six times during the season, three at home and three away.

QUEEN'S PARK

		Home		Away	
Montrose	4 pts	Won 11/8	–	Won 6/1	Lost 6/4
East Stirling	3 pts	Won 6/4	–	Drew 7/4	Lost 6/4
Berwick	3 pts	Won 6/4	–	Lost 11/4	Drew 3/1
Albion	3 pts	Won 11/10	Drew 4/5	Lost 13/8	–
Stranraer	2 pts	Drew 11/10	–	Drew 9/2	Lost 4/1
Arbroath	2 pts	Lost 11/8	Won 7/4	Lost 5/2	–
Stenhousemuir	2 pts	Drew 11/8	–	Lost 5/2	Drew 7/2
Alloa	2 pts	Lost 5/4	Drew 13/8	Drew 7/2	–
Forfar	1 pt	Lost 7/4	–	Lost 9/2	Drew 6/1
East Fife	1 pt	Lost 6/4	Drew 13/8	Lost 7/2	–
Queen O.T.S.	1 pt	Lost 11/8	Drew 11/8	Lost 5/2	–

Correct Scores

Queen's Park shared four goals three times at Hampden Park. The opponents were East Fife, Alloa and Stenhousemuir. They also drew 2-2 at both East Stirling and Forfar.

STENHOUSEMUIR

		Home		Away	
Montrose	6 pts	Won 11/8	–	Won 7/2	Won 6/4
Albion	5 pts	Won 5/4	–	Drew 6/5	Won 11/10
Queen O.T.S.	5 pts	Drew 4/6	Won 5/6	Won 5/2	–
Queen's Park	4 pts	Won 5/6	Drew 8/13	Drew 6/4	–
East Stirling	4 pts	Lost 8/11	Won 8/13	Won 15/8	–
East Fife	3 pts	Won 11/10	–	Drew 7/2	Lost 2/1
Berwick	2 pts	Lost 1/1	Drew 10/11	Drew 11/8	–
Forfar	2 pts	Won 5/4	–	Lost 4/1	Lost 10/3
Alloa	2 pts	Lost 1/1	–	Lost 7/2	Won 12/5
Stranraer	1 pt	Lost 11/8	Lost 9/2	Drew 10/3	–
Arbroath	0 pts	Lost 1/1	–	Lost 2/1	Lost 11/4

Correct Scores

Stenhousemuir won 2-0 in five home matches.

They drew 2-2 at both Brechin and Queen's Park.

STRANRAER

		Home		Away	
Montrose	6 pts	Won 4/6	–	Won 3/1	Won 4/9
East Stirling	5 pts	Won 8/13	Drew 4/7	Won 11/8	–
East Fife	5 pts	Won 5/4	–	Won 6/4	Drew 6/4
Stenhousemuir	5 pts	Drew 4/6	–	Won 11/8	Won 4/9
Albion	4 pts	Drew 8/13	–	Drew 1/1	Won 1/1
Arbroath	4 pts	Won 4/6	–	Won 11/10	Lost 11/8
Queen's Park	4 pts	Drew 8/15	Won 4/7	Drew 2/1	–
Berwick	4 pts	Lost 1/2	Won 2/9	Won 11/8	–
Forfar	4 pts	Won 11/10	Won 1/1	Lost 5/2	–
Alloa	3 pts	Lost 5/6	Drew 4/6	Won 15/8	–
Queen O.T.S.	2 pts	Drew 10/11	–	Lost 6/5	Drew 11/10

Correct Scores:-

Stranraer drew eight games 1-1 throughout the season with an even split between home and away.

They drew 2-2 with Queen of the South at Stair Park, and also drew 3-3 with Alloa at home and Queen of the South away.

Stranraer beat Montrose, Forfar and Berwick by three goals to one at home, whilst they won 4-1 on three occasions. Two of those wins were away at Alloa and Arbroath, whilst they beat East Stirling at home.

Adjusted Tables

These tables are compiled to help you evaluate form between clubs who will be facing each other again in the leagues this year.

The number of points that each club took from the promoted and relegated teams of last season has been deducted. Hence you are left with the total number of points each club gained against clubs that they will be competing with again, this season.

You will no doubt deduce that teams that feature higher on the right hand table (adjusted table), actually performed better against these same clubs than you might have supposed. If your team is higher on the left hand table (end of season), they were possibly flattered by their finishing position in the league. Certainly they will not be value for money in the early weeks of the season.

PREMIER DIVISION

END OF SEASON TABLE

1. Manchester United — 84 pts
2. Aston Villa — 74 pts
3. Norwich — 72 pts
4. Blackburn — 71 pts
5. Q.P.R. — 63 pts
6. Liverpool — 59 pts
6. Sheffield Wed. — 59 pts
6. Tottenham — 59 pts
9. Manchester City — 57 pts
10. Arsenal — 56 pts
10. Chelsea — 56 pts
12. Wimbledon — 54 pts
13. Everton — 53 pts
14. Sheffield United — 52 pts
14. Coventry — 52 pts
14. Ipswich — 52 pts
17. Leeds — 51 pts
18. Southampton — 50 pts
19. Oldham — 49 pts

ADJUSTED TABLE

1. Manchester United — 68 pts
2. Blackburn — 63 pts
3. Aston Villa — 59 pts
4. Norwich — 58 pts
5. Q.P.R. — 55 pts
6. Manchester City — 51 pts
6. Tottenham — 51 pts
8. Liverpool — 48 pts
8. Sheffield Wed. — 48 pts
10. Chelsea — 47 pts
11. Arsenal — 46 pts
11. Leeds — 46 pts
13. Sheffield United — 45 pts
14. Wimbledon — 44 pts
14. Ipswich — 44 pts
16. Coventry — 43 pts
17. Everton — 40 pts
18. Southampton — 38 pts
18. Oldham — 38 pts

FIRST DIVISION

END OF SEASON TABLE

3.	Portsmouth	88 pts
4.	Tranmere	79 pts
6.	Leicester	76 pts
7.	Millwall	70 pts
8.	Derby	66 pts
9.	Grimsby	64 pts
10.	Peterborough	62 pts
11.	Wolves	61 pts
11.	Charlton	61 pts
13.	Barnsley	60 pts
14.	Oxford	56 pts
14.	Bristol City	56 pts
16.	Watford	55 pts
17.	Notts County	52 pts
17.	Southend	52 pts
19.	Birmingham	51 pts
19.	Luton	51 pts
21.	Sunderland	50 pts

ADJUSTED TABLE

1.	Portsmouth	67 pts
2.	Leicester	60 pts
3.	Tranmere	58 pts
4.	Millwall	56 pts
5.	Peterborough	52 pts
6.	Bristol City	48 pts
6.	Wolves	48 pts
8.	Grimsby	47 pts
9.	Derby	45 pts
9.	Sunderland	45 pts
11.	Watford	40 pts
12.	Birmingham	39 pts
12.	Charlton	39 pts
12.	Notts County	39 pts
12.	Oxford	39 pts
16.	Barnsley	38 pts
17.	Southend	37 pts
18.	Luton	36 pts

The end of season table simply excludes the teams that were promoted and relegated last season.

The adjusted table is the finishing order in points totals, with the points gained against the promoted and relegated clubs having been subtracted.

This is therefore a table between the teams that will once again contest the first division this season.

In all cases the goal difference has been ignored.

SECOND DIVISION

END OF SEASON TABLE

3.	Port Vale	89 pts
5.	Swansea	73 pts
6.	Stockport	72 pts
6.	Leyton Orient	72 pts
8.	Brighton	69 pts
8.	Reading	69 pts
10.	Bradford	68 pts
11.	Fulham	65 pts
11.	Rotherham	65 pts
13.	Burnley	61 pts
14.	Plymouth	60 pts
14.	Huddersfield	60 pts
16.	Hartlepool	54 pts
17.	Bournemouth	53 pts
18.	Blackpool	51 pts
19.	Exeter	50 pts
19.	Hull	50 pts

ADJUSTED TABLE

1.	Port Vale	61 pts
2.	Swansea	53 pts
3.	Reading	51 pts
4.	Leyton Orient	48 pts
5.	Rotherham	47 pts
5.	Stockport	47 pts
7.	Burnley	46 pts
8.	Bradford	44 pts
9.	Fulham	41 pts
10.	Brighton	40 pts
10.	Huddersfield	40 pts
12.	Hull	39 pts
13.	Bournemouth	38 pts
13.	Hartlepool	38 pts
15.	Exeter	33 pts
16.	Blackpool	32 pts
17.	Plymouth	30 pts

THIRD DIVISION

END OF SEASON TABLE

5.	Walsall	73 pts
6.	Crew	70 pts
7.	Bury	63 pts
7.	Lincoln	63 pts
9.	Shrewsbury	62 pts
10.	Colchester	59 pts
11.	Rochdale	58 pts
12.	Chesterfield	56 pts
13.	Scarborough	54 pts
13.	Scunthorpe	54 pts
15.	Darlington	50 pts
16.	Doncaster	47 pts
17.	Hereford	45 pts
18.	Carlisle	44 pts
19.	Torquay	43 pts
20.	Northampton	41 pts
21.	Gillingham	40 pts

ADJUSTED TABLE

1.	Walsall	60 pts
2.	Crewe	54 pts
3.	Colchester	52 pts
3.	Lincoln	52 pts
5.	Rochdale	51 pts
6.	Shrewsbury	50 pts
7.	Bury	49 pts
8.	Chesterfield	47 pts
9.	Scarborough	43 pts
9.	Scunthorpe	43 pts
11.	Darlington	42 pts
12.	Doncaster	39 pts
13.	Carlisle	38 pts
14.	Hereford	35 pts
15.	Northampton	33 pts
16.	Gillingham	32 pts
17.	Torquay	30 pts

SCOTTISH PREMIER DIVISION

END OF SEASON TABLE

1.	Rangers	73 pts
2.	Aberdeen	64 pts
3.	Celtic	60 pts
4.	Dundee United	47 pts
5.	Hearts	44 pts
6.	St. Johnstone	40 pts
7.	Hibernian	37 pts
8.	Partick	36 pts
9.	Motherwell	35 pts
10.	Dundee	34 pts

ADJUSTED TABLE

1.	Rangers	59 pts
2.	Aberdeen	51 pts
3.	Celtic	45 pts
4.	Hearts	38 pts
5.	Dundee United	33 pts
6.	Hibernian	30 pts
7.	Partick	29 pts
8.	St. Johnstone	27 pts
9.	Dundee	26 pts
10.	Motherwell	22 pts

SCOTTISH FIRST DIVISION

END OF SEASON TABLE

3.	Dunfermline	52 pts
4.	St. Mirren	51 pts
5.	Hamilton	50 pts
6.	Morton	48 pts
7.	Ayr	46 pts
8.	Clydebank	45 pts
9.	Dumbarton	37 pts
10.	Stirling	35 pts

ADJUSTED TABLE

1.	St. Mirren	34 pts
2.	Dunfermline	32 pts
3.	Ayr	31 pts
3.	Hamilton	31 pts
5.	Morton	29 pts
6.	Dumbarton	25 pts
7.	Clydebank	24 pts
8.	Stirling	18 pts

SCOTTISH SECOND DIVISION

END OF SEASON TABLE			**ADJUSTED TABLE**		
3.	Stranraer	53 pts	1.	Stranraer	46 pts
4.	Forfar	46 pts	2.	Forfar	41 pts
5.	Alloa	44 pts	3.	Alloa	40 pts
5.	Arbroath	44 pts	3.	Arbroath	40 pts
7.	Stenhousemuir	40 pts	5.	Berwick	37 pts
8.	Berwick	39 pts	6.	East Fife	34 pts
9.	East Fife	38 pts	6.	Stenhousemuir	34 pts
10.	Queen O.T.S.	33 pts	8.	Queen O.T.S.	30 pts
11.	Queen's Park	28 pts	9.	East Stirling	24 pts
12.	Montrose	27 pts	9.	Montrose	24 pts
13.	East Stirling	25 pts	9.	Queen's Park	24 pts
14.	Albion	22 pts	12.	Albion	22 pts

Level Stake Betting

In this part of the book, we endeavour to show you that a profit can be made from the fixed odds coupons, particularly from level stake betting.

The returns you will find on the following pages are approximate, and are based on a one pound level stake throughout the season.

Odds vary from bookmaker to bookmaker, but generally they even out over the course of a season.

The larger profits usually come from the more exaggerated scorelines, and you should perhaps concentrate on the more frequent scores to larger stakes.

By all means though, back your fancy provided there are repetitive results occurring to back up your judgement.

Remain objective at all times, and always consider that it may take months to obtain your profit on the bet. For that reason alone we repeat a saying we mentioned earlier, "bet within your means".

Teams quoted are those who have not changed leagues this year due to promotion or relegation.

Team by team Level Stake Profit Betting for Last Season:
Teams quoted are those who have not changed leagues this year
due to promotion or relegation.

Betting at one pound level stakes

PREMIER DIVISION

Arsenal	Lose all matches 0-1 home and away	+ £35.00
Aston Villa	Win 3-2 in all away matches	+ £37.00
Blackburn	Win 4-1 in all home matches Plus Mike Newell to be first goalscorer.	+ £59.00
Chelsea	Lose 2-4 in all matches home and away	+ £28.00
Coventry	Win all home matches by 3-0	+ £27.00
Everton	Win all matches 3-0 both home and away	+ £65.00
Ipswich	Lose away matches by 0-3	+ £22.00
Leeds	Lose all away matches by 0-4	+ £71.00
Liverpool	Draw 2-2 in all away matches	+ £24.00
Manchester City	Lose 1-3 in all away matches Plus David White to be first goalscorer	+ £24.00
Manchester United	Win 3-0 in all home matches Plus Mark Hughes to be first goalscorer	+ £16.00
Norwich	Win all away matches 3-2	+ £81.00
Oldham	Draw 2-2 in all matches both home and away	+ £18.00
	Plus lose 0-2 in all away matches	+ £20.50
Q.P.R.	Win all home matches by 3-1	+ £32.00
Sheffield Utd.	Lose 0-2 in all home matches	+ £20.50
Sheffield Wed.	Draw 1-1 in all matches home and away Plus Mark Bright to be first goalscorer	+ £24.50
Southampton	Draw all home matches 2-2	+ £ 9.00
Tottenham	Lose all away matches 1-4 Plus Teddy Sheringham to be first goalscorer	+ £59.00
Wimbledon	Win all matches 3-2 both home and away	+ £42.00

FIRST DIVISION

Barnsley	Win all home matches 1-0	+ £18.00
Birmingham	Draw all away games 0-0	+ £15.00
Bristol City	Draw 0-0 in all matches both home/away	+ £26.00
Charlton	Lose all away matches by 0-1	+ £16.00
Derby	Win all away matches by 3-1	+ £17.00
Grimsby	Lose all away matches by 1-2	+ £25.00
Leicester	Win all away games 3-1	+ £53.00
Luton	Draw all home matches 0-0	+ £34.00
Millwall	Lose 0-3 in all away matches	+ £43.00
Notts County	Draw 2-2 or 3-3 in all away games	+ £86.00
Oxford	Win 1-0 in all away games	+ £25.00
Peterborough	Draw 1-1 in all home games	+ £22.50
Portsmouth	Win 4-0 in all home games Plus Whittingham or Mc Loughlin to be first goalscorer	+ £90.00
Southend	Win all home matches by 3-0	+ £44.00
Sunderland	Lose 1-2 in all games both home and away	+ £18.00
Tranmere	Win 4-0 in all their home matches	+ £52.00
Watford	Draw 0-0 in all home matches	+ £22.00
Wolves	Win 3-0 in all their home matches	+ £23.00

SECOND DIVISION

Blackpool	Draw 2-2 or 3-3 in all matches home and away	+ £79.00
Bournemouth	Draw all their matches 1-1 home or away	+ £19.00
Bradford	Win 3-1 in all their home matches	+ £28.00
Brighton	Win or lose 3-2 in all their matches	+ £44.00
Burnley	Draw all their matches 1-1 home and away	+ £25.50
Exeter	Draw 2-2 in all matches home and away	+ £44.00
Fulham	Draw 1-1 in all matches home and away	+ £13.50
Hartlepool	Lose 0-3 in all their away matches	+ £29.00
Huddersfield	Win or Lose 2-1 in all games home or away	+ £20.00
Hull	Lose all their away games by 0-3	+ £31.00
Leyton Orient	Win 3-2 in home matches	+ £29.00
Plymouth	Win 2-1 in all their home games	+ £13.00
Port Vale	Draw 2-2 in all home games	+ £22.00
Reading	Win 4-0 in all home matches Plus 1-1 in all away games	+ £59.00 + £16.00
Rotherham	Win or lose 3-2 in all home games	+ £63.00
Stockport	Draw 2-2 in all games either home or away	+ £44.00
Swansea	Win 3-0 in all home games	+ £20.00

THIRD DIVISION

Bury	Draw 3-3 at home in all their matches	+ £60.00
Carlisle	Draw 2-2 away from home in all matches	+ £39.00
Chesterfield	Win 2-1 at home in all their matches	+ £33.00
Colchester	Lose 1-3 away from home	+ £47.00
Crewe	Win 4-0 at home in all matches	+ £49.00
Darlington	Win 3-0 away from home	+ £113.00
Doncaster	Draw 1-1 away from home	+ £24.50
Gillingham	Draw 1-1 away from home	+ £24.50
Hereford	Draw 1-1 in all matches both at home and away	+ £36.00
Lincoln	Win 2-1 in all matches home or away	+ £14.00
Northampton	Lose 0-2 in all matches home and away	+ £10.50
Rochdale	Draw 1-1 in all away games	+ £10.50
Scarborough	Draw 2-2 in all home matches	+ £24.00
Scunthorpe	Draw 2-2 in all games at home and away	+ £33.00
Shrewsbury	Win or lose 3-2 in all home games	+ £52.00
Torquay	Draw 2-2 in all games both home and away	+ £33.00
Walsall	Win either 3-1 or 3-2 in all home games	+ £78.00

SCOTTISH PREMIER DIVISION

Aberdeen	Win 2-1 in all their away games	+ £25.50
Celtic	Draw 1-1 in all their away games	+ £17.00
Dundee	Draw 0-0 in all away matches	+ £16.00
Dundee United	Win 1-0 away in all games	+ £14.00
Hearts	Win 1-0 in all home matches	+ £34.00
Hibernian	Win 3-1 at home	+ £38.00
	Plus draw 2-2 at home	+ £23.00
Motherwell	Lose 1-3 in all home games	+ £38.00
Partick	Draw 2-2 in all matches home and away	+ £16.00
Rangers	Win 4-1 away from home	+ £33.00
St. Johnstone	Draw 1-1 in all matches home and away	+ £34.00
	Plus draw 2-2 in all away matches	+ £23.00

SCOTTISH FIRST DIVISION

Ayr	Draw 0-0 in all home matches	+ £27.50
	Plus draw 1-1 in all away games	+ £23.50
Clydebank	Draw 3-3 in all away games	+ £80.00
	Plus win 3-1 in all home matches	+ £29.00
Dumbarton	Lose 2-3 in all away games	+ £33.00
Dunfermline	Lose 1-3 in all home matches	+ £60.00
Hamilton	Lose 1-3 in all home matches	+ £60.00
Morton	Draw 2-2 in all away matches	+ £23.00
Stirling	Win 2-1 in all home matches	+ £18.00
St. Mirren	Win 2-1 in all away games	+ £28.00

234

SCOTTISH SECOND DIVISION

Albion	Lose 2-0 in all away games	+ £20.50
Alloa	Lose 0-2 in all home games	+ £46.00
	Plus draw 2-2 in all away games	+ £23.00
Arbroath	Win 3-1 in all away games	+ £33.00
	Plus draw 0-0 in all home games	+ £27.50
Berwick	Win 3-1 in all away games	+ £111.00
East Fife	Draw 2-2 in all matches at home or away	+ £36.00
East Stirling	Lose 1-4 or 1-5 in all away games	+ £154.00
	Plus lose 1-2 in all home games	+ £30.00
Forfar	Win or lose 3-2 away from home	+ £18.00
Montrose	Lose 1-3 in all away games	+ £52.00
Queen of the South	Lose 1-5 in all away games	+ £129.00
Queen's Park	Draw 2-2 in all matches home and away	+ £36.00
Stenhousemuir	Win 2-0 at home in all games	+ £35.00
Stranraer	Draw 3-3 in all games home and away	+ £63.00
	Plus draw 1-1 in all matches, home and away	+ £13.00

Premier League level stake returns

On these pages you will find a one pound level stake return for individual teams in the Premier Division.

We list these for interest only, as usually you cannot bet in singles outside of televised matches.

It is significant that only six teams give a profit over the course of a season, and that Norwich City come out on top of the league.

Bookmakers continued to underestimate 'The Canaries' until late on in the season. It remains to be seen if they can follow up with another good year. If Mark Robins remains fit, they could yet surprise more people.

As usual Wimbledon's position in the league is interesting. Whatever you say about them, Wimbledon always seem to create interest and usually upset the form book just when you leeast expect it to happen.

Premier League

	HOME			AWAY	
1	Norwich	+£4.18	1	Everton	+£6. 78
2	Blackburn	+£4.10	2	Norwich	+£6.54
3	Oldham	+£3.50	3	Man. Utd.	+£2.82
4	Q.P.R .	+£2.83	4	Coventry	+£2.22
5	Liverpool	+£2.70	5	Man. City	+£1.99
6	Tottenham	+£2.65	6	Wimbledon	+£1.18
7	Southampton	+£2.45	7	C. Palace	−£0.24
8	Aston Villa	+£2.39	8	Aston Villa	−£0.91
9	Man. Utd.	+£2.04	9	Blackburn	−£1.89
10	Leeds	+£1.69	10	Arsenal	−£3.76
11	Sheffield U.	+£0.81	11	Q.P.R.	−£3.93
12	Wimbledon	+£0.73	12	Sheffield W.	−£4.84
13	Chelsea	−£1.89	13	Tottenham	−£4.95
14	Ipswich	−£2.11	14	Nottm. Forest	−£5.00
15	Middlesbrough	−£2.30	15	Chelsea	−£5.20

16	Sheffield W.	−£3.38	16	Oldham	−£5.40
17	Coventry	−£4.62	17	Sheffield U.	−£7.78
18	Everton	−£4.95	18	Ipswich	−£8.00
19	Arsenal	−£6.55	19	Middlesbro	−£8.42
20	Man. City	−£6.87	20	Southampton	−£11.15
21	Nottm. Forest	−£7.31	21	Liverpool	−£12.00
22	C. Palace	−£7.50	22	Leeds	−£21. 00

IN TOTAL

1	Norwich	+£10.72
2	Manchester United	+£4.86
3	Blackburn	+£2.21
4	Wimbledon	+£1.91
5	Everton	+£1.83
6	Aston Villa	+£1.48
7	Q.P.R.	−£1.10
8	Oldham	−£1.90
9	Tottenham	−£2.30
10	Coventry	−£2.40
11	Man. City	−£4.88
12	Sheffield United	−£6.97
13	Chelsea	−£7.09
14	Crystal Palace	−£7.74
15	Sheffield Wednesday	−£8.22
16	Southampton	−£8.70
17	Liverpool	−£9.30
18	Ipswich	−£10.11
19	Arsenal	−£10.31
20	Middlesbrough	−£10.72
21	Nottingham Forest	−£12.31
22	Leeds United	−£19.31

Statistics

There are people in life who will tell you that figures can say what you want them to say.

I suppose there is a certain amount of truth in that, but it remains a negative response to me.

I prefer to think that figures never lie.

The first page in this section should prove my point. You cannot argue with the figures, and if Steve Coppell and the Palace supporters still believe they were unlucky to be relegated, they should peruse this list!

The following page lists the relevant first goalscorers for their respective clubs. We have only drawn up the premier division teams, as in most cases, this is where the bulk of the betting is done.

This does not have to be the case nowadays though.

Your local bookmaker should accomodate you if you require a first goalscorer bet, provided the match in questions fits in with the current betting rules.

For this reason, we have listed first goalscorers in the 'team by team' chapter.

The following statistics are then listed in divisional order.

The number of times a team in the Premier Division scored the opening goal of a game

It is a fact that around two thirds of the teams that score the first goal of the game go on to win the match.

When you are betting on the first goalscorer, it is essential that you refer to a list such as this, otherwise you are betting completely in the dark.

Home		Away		Totals	
Blackburn	16	Manchester Utd	12	Blackburn	27
Oldham	14	Aston Villa	11	Aston Villa	23
Leeds	13	Blackburn	11	Sheffield Wed.	23
Sheffield Utd	13	Manchester City	11	Manchester Utd	22
Sheffield Wed.	13	Sheffield Wed.	10	Liverpool	21
Aston Villa	12	Southampton	10	Manchester City	21
Chelsea	12	Coventry	9	Southampton	21
Liverpool	12	Everton	9	Coventry	20
Coventry	11	Ipswich	9	Norwich	20
Norwich	11	Liverpool	9	Chelsea	19
Southampton	11	Middlesborugh	9	Oldham	19
Wimbledon	11	Norwich	9	Sheffield Utd	19
Arsenal	10	Arsenal	8	Wimbledon	19
Manchester City	10	Tottenham	8	Arsenal	18
Manchester Utd	10	Wimbledon	8	Ipswich	18
Tottenham	10	Chelsea	7	Leeds	18
Ipswich	9	Crystal Palace	7	Tottenham	18
Q.P.R.	9	Q.P.R.	7	Everton	16
Crystal Palace	8	Nott'g'm Forest	6	Middlesbrough	16
Everton	7	Sheffield Utd	6	Q.P.R.	16
Middlesbrough	7	Leeds	5	Crystal Palace	15
Nott'g'm Forest	7	Oldham	5	Nott'g'm Forest	13

The bottom two places speak for themselves, whilst Middlesbrough who joined the others in being relegated are joint third bottom.

If you look on the relevant page you will see that Blackburn provided the top pairing of first goalscorers.

That is hardly surprising when you study these lists.

Players who scored the opening goal in a Premier League game – club by club – minimum 3 occasions

Arsenal:	Wright (5) Merson (3) Smith (3)
Aston Villa:	Yorke (4) Saunders (4) Parker (4) Atkinson (3)
Blackburn:	Newell (8) Shearer (6) Wilcox (3) Ripley (3)
Chelsea:	Harford (5) Stuart (5)
Coventry:	Williams (5) Quinn (5)
Crystal Palace:	Armstrong (6)
Everton:	Beardsley (4) Cottee (3)
Ipswich:	Kiwomba (5) Johnson (4)
Leeds:	Chapman (3) McCallister (3)
Liverpool:	Hutchison (4) Walters (4) Rush (4) Barnes (3) Rosenthal (3)
Manchester City:	White (8) Quinn (4) Sheron (3) Flitcroft (3)
Manchester Utd:	Hughes (7) Ince (4) Giggs (4)
Middlesbrough:	Wilkinson (4) Falconer (3)
Norwich:	Robins (4)
Nottingham Fst:	Clough (4)
Oldham:	Henry (3)
Q.P.R:	Ferdinand (6) Allen (4)
Sheffield Utd:	Deane (4) Littlejohn (4) Carr (3)
Sheffield Wed:	Bright (7) Hirst (4) Warhurst (4)
Southampton:	LeTissier (5) Dowie (4) Maddison (3) Banger (3)
Tottenham:	Sheringham (7)
Wimbledon:	Holdsworth (5) Fashanu (3)

P.S. If you don't think these charts are worthwhile and/or that bookmakers never make mistakes look at the Oldham list. When Nick Henry scored the goal at Aston Villa, he was a 25/1 chance to do so!
That was the third time that he had scored the opening goal of the game in a three month period.

PREMIER DIVISION

	Number of times a team won by only one goal.			Number of times a team lost by only one goal.			Number of times a team won by two goals or more.			Number of times a team lost by two goals or more.		
	H	A	T	H	A	T	H	A	T	H	A	T
Arsenal	4	5	9	5	7	12	4	2	6	2	2	4
Aston Villa	5	7	12	2	4	6	8	1	9	1	3	4
Blackburn	6	3	9	2	5	7	7	4	11	2	2	4
Chelsea	6	4	10	3	4	7	3	1	4	2	5	7
Coventry	3	3	6	6	2	8	4	3	7	4	4	8
Everton	4	4	8	3	7	10	3	4	7	5	4	9
Ipswich	5	2	7	4	4	8	3	2	5	0	6	6
Leeds	4	0	4	0	5	5	8	0	8	1	9	10
Liverpool	7	3	10	3	6	9	6	0	6	1	5	6
Man. City	3	4	7	5	5	10	4	4	8	1	4	5
Man. Utd	6	5	11	1	4	5	8	5	13	1	0	1
Norwich	10	6	16	0	2	2	3	2	5	2	8	10
Oldham	5	3	8	5	5	10	5	0	5	0	9	9
Q.P.R.	5	4	9	2	7	9	6	2	8	3	1	4
Sheff. Utd	4	1	5	3	6	9	6	3	9	2	7	9
Sheff Weds	5	4	9	3	6	9	4	2	6	1	3	4
S'th'pton	7	3	10	5	8	13	3	0	3	0	5	5
Tottenham	4	2	6	2	3	5	7	3	10	3	7	10
Wimbledon	3	4	7	6	4	10	6	1	7	2	4	6

This table probably shows that Manchester City, in particular, had a better season than most people gave them credit for. Manchester United obviously had a great season, and our figures prove them to be worthy champions.

FIRST DIVISION

	Number of times a team won by only one goal.			Number of times a team lost by only one goal.			Number of times a team won by two goals or more.			Number of times a team lost by two goals or more.		
	H	A	T	H	A	T	H	A	T	H	A	T
Barnsley	7	2	9	6	7	13	5	3	8	1	6	7
Birmingham	7	1	8	4	5	9	3	2	5	5	7	12
Bristol City	8	3	11	4	5	9	2	1	3	2	7	9
Charlton	5	3	8	3	9	12	5	3	8	2	3	5
Derby	4	2	6	8	7	15	7	6	13	2	1	3
Grimsby	8	3	11	1	11	12	4	4	8	4	4	8
Leicester	8	3	11	3	1	4	6	5	11	1	9	10
Luton	1	3	4	0	6	6	5	1	6	4	5	9
Millwall	6	3	9	1	3	4	8	1	9	2	6	8
Notts Cnty	4	0	4	3	3	6	6	2	8	3	9	12
Oxford	3	5	8	7	4	11	5	1	6	1	6	7
Peterboro'	5	7	12	3	5	8	2	2	4	2	6	8
Portsmouth	7	4	11	2	3	5	12	3	15	0	5	5
Southend	3	2	5	4	5	9	6	2	8	2	9	11
Sunderland	3	4	7	5	9	14	6	0	6	3	5	8
Tranmere	6	6	12	1	4	5	9	2	11	3	5	8
Watford	5	5	10	5	5	10	3	1	4	3	6	9
Wolves	7	3	10	4	4	8	4	2	6	2	7	9

The statistics for Derby and Portsmouth are outstanding.
Of the other clubs, Barnsley and Sunderland fared better than
you would have imagined.

SECOND DIVISION

	Number of times a team won by only one goal.			Number of times a team lost by only one goal.			Number of times a team won by two goals or more.			Number of times a team lost by two goals or more.		
	H	A	T	H	A	T	H	A	T	H	A	T
Blackpool	2	3	5	2	8	10	7	0	7	3	6	9
Bournem'th	4	4	8	3	7	10	3	1	4	4	4	8
Bradford	6	5	11	4	2	6	6	2	8	2	6	8
Brighton	6	5	11	2	6	8	7	2	9	4	5	9
Burnley	4	2	6	2	4	6	7	2	9	2	7	9
Exeter	1	2	3	7	0	7	4	4	8	3	8	11
Fulham	6	4	10	3	5	8	3	3	6	2	3	5
Hartlepool	5	2	7	4	2	6	3	4	7	5	9	14
Huddersf'ld	7	5	12	6	8	14	3	2	5	1	5	6
Hull	6	4	10	5	2	7	3	0	3	4	11	15
Leyton Or'nt	7	1	8	3	5	8	9	4	13	0	8	8
Plymouth	6	2	8	4	4	8	5	3	8	2	8	10
Port Vale	3	8	11	1	4	5	11	4	15	1	3	4
Reading	5	3	8	4	3	7	9	1	10	1	5	6
Rotherham	6	4	10	4	1	5	3	4	7	3	7	10
Stockport	1	4	5	1	6	7	10	4	14	0	5	5
Swansea	4	4	8	4	4	8	8	4	12	0	5	5

Huddersfield's matches were obviously close run affairs, whilst Stockport were a little unfortunate not to finish higher in the league according to these figures.

THIRD DIVISION

	Number of times a team won by only one goal.			Number of times a team lost by only one goal.			Number of times a team won by two goals or more.			Number of times a team lost by two goals or more.		
	H	A	T	H	A	T	H	A	T	H	A	T
Bury	4	6	10	3	5	8	6	2	8	1	6	7
Carlisle	2	2	4	5	6	11	5	2	7	4	5	9
Chesterfield	9	2	11	4	6	10	2	2	4	3	3	6
Colchester	6	2	8	1	6	7	7	3	10	4	8	12
Crewe	5	6	11	4	5	9	8	2	10	1	4	5
Darlington	2	3	5	5	2	7	3	4	7	5	4	9
Doncaster	6	4	10	9	2	11	0	1	1	1	5	6
Gillingham	2	0	2	5	5	10	7	0	7	3	7	10
Hereford	2	2	4	1	3	4	5	1	6	4	9	13
Lincoln	5	5	10	4	4	8	5	3	8	1	6	7
North'pton	5	3	8	5	5	10	1	2	3	5	8	13
Rochdale	4	4	8	6	1	7	6	2	8	2	7	9
Scarborough	2	4	6	4	5	9	5	4	9	3	6	9
Scunthorpe	0	4	4	4	6	10	8	2	10	2	4	6
Shrewsbury	8	3	11	6	4	10	3	3	6	1	3	4
Torquay	5	4	9	7	5	12	1	2	3	4	7	11
Walsall	6	6	12	3	4	7	5	5	10	1	5	6

Scunthorpe's figures make impressive reading, and it is hard to fathom how they finished so far down the league. They could be the surprise package of the third division this year.

SCOTTISH PREMIER DIVISION

	Number of times a team won by only one goal.			Number of times a team lost by only one goal.			Number of times a team won by two goals or more.			Number of times a team lost by two goals or more.		
	H	A	T	H	A	T	H	A	T	H	A	T
Aberdeen	5	6	11	2	3	5	8	8	16	0	2	2
Celtic	7	9	16	4	2	6	6	2	8	0	2	2
Dundee	5	2	7	6	5	11	2	2	4	5	5	10
Dundee Utd	5	6	11	4	6	10	3	5	8	3	3	6
Hearts	9	1	10	3	7	10	3	2	5	1	4	5
Hibernian	4	2	6	4	6	10	4	2	6	2	7	9
Motherwell	3	2	5	4	6	10	4	2	6	7	3	10
Rangers	7	7	14	0	3	3	13	6	19	0	1	1
St. J'nst'ne	3	1	4	0	4	4	5	1	6	4	6	10

Perhaps Celtic and Aberdeen should join forces to stop Rangers' domination in the league. Celtic's battling performances to win by the odd goal coupled with Aberdeen's record of winning games by two goals or more, could just add some spice to events this season!

SCOTTISH FIRST AND SECOND DIVISIONS

	Number of times a team won by only one goal.			Number of times a team lost by only one goal.			Number of times a team won by two goals or more.			Number of times a team lost by two goals or more.		
	H	A	T	H	A	T	H	A	T	H	A	T
Ayr	5	2	7	3	5	8	4	3	7	1	3	4
Clydebank	1	3	4	3	4	7	9	3	12	1	7	8
Dumbarton	5	4	9	5	8	13	5	1	6	4	5	9
Dunf'mline	5	9	14	4	6	10	5	3	8	3	1	4
Hamilton	5	3	8	1	7	8	6	5	11	3	2	5
Morton	6	4	10	6	2	8	5	4	9	2	5	7
Stirling	5	2	7	6	6	12	2	2	4	4	4	8
St. Mirren	7	7	14	5	3	8	4	3	7	1	5	6

Hamilton finished only fifth last year, but they were only two wins away from a promotion place. These figures would suggest that they will be there or thereabouts again this season.

	H	A	T	H	A	T	H	A	T	H	A	T
Albion	3	1	4	5	4	9	1	1	2	5	9	14
Alloa	4	4	8	0	1	1	4	4	8	7	3	10
Arbroath	4	6	10	4	2	6	4	4	8	2	5	7
Berwick	3	2	5	2	1	3	5	6	11	4	9	13
East Fife	3	1	4	5	2	7	3	7	10	3	5	8
East Stirl'g	1	3	4	6	3	9	3	1	4	6	7	13
Forfar	3	4	7	2	4	6	7	4	11	2	3	5
Montrose	1	4	5	3	2	5	4	1	5	9	8	17
Q'n of t' S'th	1	4	5	8	3	11	4	3	7	3	4	7
Queen's Park	3	1	4	4	5	9	3	1	4	3	7	10
Stenh'sem'r	1	2	3	3	5	8	8	4	12	5	1	6
Stranraer	2	6	8	1	1	2	6	5	11	1	2	3

Stranraer, Forfar and perhaps Stenhousemuir should be the teams fighting for honours this time around.

A View on Promoted Sides in All Divisions

The forecasting of results for promoted (or relegated sides) in the first few weeks of a season is always difficult.

I tend to stick with teams who have retained the same management by and large because their pattern of play will be similar to that of the previous season.

Ipswich Town were probably a good example last season of how hard it is to assess promoted sides. Ipswich were probably the least fancied of the three promoted teams to the Premier Division, yet it was they who started so well along with Blackburn Rovers who only went up via the play-off system.

Ipswich did 'the double' over Wimbledon (no mean achievement) in the first few weeks of the season , and held their own against the likes of Tottenham, Liverpool, Aston Villa and Manchester United. They eventually lost to Oldham of all people, thus illustrating how difficult forecasting is.

If you must include such sides in your early season fixed odds coupons, stick to promoted sides rather than relegated teams. It is unlikely that teams that have made 'the drop' will retain the same management team, so it follows that their respective matches are going to be difficult to forecast.

For the same reasons, I would give the likes of Swindon Town and West Bromwich Albion a wide berth in the early part of the coming season. They have both lost their respective managers to supposedly more illustrious clubs, and are both going to struggle in the first few weeks of the season in my opinion. West Brom have been quoted at 14/1 or thereabouts for the first division, but I wouldn't back them at fifties until I saw some kind of early success come August.

Let us take a look then at each of the divisions in turn.

Premier League

We have already touched on Swindon, and I have to wonder how they are going to react to the loss of Glenn Hoddle. His management skills are unknown to most of us, but there is no denying that he was the difference between success and failure on the field in many of last seasons fixtures. I wish them well, but it will be a mighty achievement just to stay in the top flight. They look worth opposing in their first few fixtures, though they seem to have been fortunate in that they do not face a particularly difficult start on paper. Although they face Liverpool at home in their third match, it is not until late September that they face their first gruelling away fixture at Old Trafford. Their first match is away at Sheffield United, and it is worth remembering that Manchester United came unstuck at Brammel Lane in the opening match last year.

Newcastle United are a different team to assess entirely. Keegan and McDermott seem to be assembling the right kind of balance between youth and experience in the north-east. They have some wonderful talent coming through, though their defence would worry me.

For this reason I believe Newcastle could be worth following in the high scoring draw department. With correct odds on offer of around 14/1 for 2-2 draws, and up to 80/1 for 3-3 results, Newcastle could be the team to include in such wagers.

They scored the first goal in twenty eight of their forty six league fixtures last term, but will find it tough going this time around. Given their massive scoring potential, I could see Newcastle successfully 'chasing' games and high scoring matches are a definite possibility.

Talking of their attack, Keegan has made a shrewd move in letting David Kelly move on. Kelly was an inspiration last season, but it has to be said that the first division is probably his niche. He was far less effective in the top flight before, and Keegan and co look to have made the correct assessment of a player who performed so well for them last year. Such management decisions are vital, and the fact that Keegan has sold Kelly is impressive. You cannot let sentiment get in the way of major decisions, and the ex-England striker looks to have all the right management skills.

Newcastle play footballing sides in the first few weeks of the season. Goals look guaranteed both ends of the field against the likes of Tottenham, Coventry and Manchester United in their first three fixtures.

Very few people deserve success as much as Billy Bonds at West Ham, but The Hammers look up against it once more in the senior league. They play Liverpool and Arsenal in two of the last three matches of the season, and their fans will be more than happy if they have achieved safety by the time they entertain Liverpool on April 23. It may well pay to oppose West Ham in their home games. When West Ham struggle, it is often in front of their own fans, and value could be obtained if you are searching for aways on your coupon.

Division One

It goes without saying that Stoke had a wonderful time of it last year. They achieved 'the double' over seven teams in the league, and Port Vale and West Brom were among those victims.

Stoke play their fellow promoted sides in Bolton and West Brom in their second and third fixtures of the season after entertaining Millwall on the opening day. This could, and perhaps should put them into a positive mood for the rest of the season. They were a team who thrived on starting well last year, and would have won the league in a canter but for dropping home points, when seemingly disinterested with meagre opposition, towards the end of the season. 'Clean sheet' victories are the forecast, with Stoke more than holding their own in this competitive league.

We have talked of West Brom already, and whilst this well supported club deserve to be playing in the upper echelons of football, I believe they could struggle.

Too many mediocre teams scored too many goals against them last year for my liking. They conceded five at home to Plymouth, whilst ten teams scored two or more against them away from The Hawthorns. They look worth opposing when playing away from home.

Bolton look difficult to assess, and I would wait for the formlines to come in before including them in any weekly wagers.

Division Two

York had a difficult period to endure before confirming promotion to the second division.

First of all they had to wait a week after they had completed their programme to see how the final table stood, and then go through the play-off matches before they finally won promotion in extra time against Crewe Alexandra.

York were the only team to beat Barnet twice last time around, winning 5-1 away from home. Clearly that sort of form would serve them well in the second division, though home defeats by Bury and Walsall (the only side they 'lost' the double to) would provoke some worry. They battled well at Wembley though, and reached a best placed 15th in the old second division back in '74-'75. Therefore they are used to playing in better divisions , and their undoubted ability to score goals will help their cause considerably.

If Barnet get over their current problems off the field, they should prove an interesting addition to the second division.

They started at odds on in nineteen of their twenty one home matches and won fourteen of them which is a good average. They also won the two other 'non odds on' games. Scoring goals was never a problem last season, though they lacked a player who regularly opened the scoring in a match.

A 'wait and see' policy should be used for Barnet, both on and off the pitch.

Cardiff were away 'bankers' last year when they were fancied to win their matches. They started 11/8 or shorter eight times on their travels and won every time. If they show any form at all early doors, it should pay to back them to win against vulnerable teams.

Wrexham lost eight matches last term and were behind by half time in all of them. They obviously lacked confidence for some reason when they fell behind, and that is a worrying statistic when a team goes up a division. It goes without saying that there is more likelihood of Wrexham being behind at the interval in a stronger league, so clearly the warning signs are there.

Wrexham featured in nine 'jackpot' draws with six of them coming away from home.

Scottish Premier Division

Raith Rovers are quoted as massive outsiders now they have reached the top flight. That is understandable enough, but I feel they have the strikers to cause their opponents trouble. Dalziel, Brester and Crawford scored the opening goal of the match on twenty one occasions between them, last season. Obviously it will be tougher now they are in with the big boys, but a team that has that many potential scorers are always in with a shout. Raith are a team destined to feature in matches which produce lots of goals.

Kilmarnock fought their way to nine 1-0 victories last term with six of them coming at home. This spirit to battle out a result will help their cause, but they conceded two goals in a game nine times away from home, and they could be on the receiving end of some heavy defeats unless they improve their form away from Rugby Park.

Scottish First Division

Clarke and McGarvey did well in the scoring department for Clyde last season. This undoubtably aided their push for promotion, and will be needed even more in the first division. Clyde were relegated in '90-'91 when they only scored 41 goals in 39 matches, so with any luck the strikers could save Clyde this time around.

Although they finished behind Clyde, Brechin beat the second division champions in all three matches last year, with two of the matches being played at Clyde. Being able to beat better opposition might enable Brechin to fare better than Clyde , though Brechin finished bottom of Division One when both teams were relegated in 1991.

RELEGATED TEAMS

To First Division

If Steve Coppel had stayed with Crystal Palace I could have strongly fancied them to have won the first division for reasons already given. Oldham won their last three matches at combined odds of around 20/1 to send Palace crashing out of the top league. Palace were the last team to win a Premier game last season, and that statistic finally caught up with them. I could see Palace drawing several games this time around in order to gain respectablility.

According to the experts Middlesbrough were doomed from the moment they won promotion to the Premier League. They duly proved the experts right despite having a reasonable start and winning some tough looking games. Division One is very much their niche though, and I could fancy them to do best of the three relegated sides,although in the bookmakers eyes they are the 'outsiders of three'.

They have shown many times that they are able to cope in this, the hardest of divisions in many ways. They are experienced enough to battle their way back and could prove value for money on a week to week basis via the fixed odds coupons. Unfashionable sides like Middlesbrough are invariably well priced and very often offer value for money.

Many people believe that Forest will bounce straight back up, and they are generally second favourites behind Derby to do just that. I have my doubts personally.

They lost 'the double' to seven teams last year including the likes of Ipswich and Everton which does not make good reading. They look another 'draw' side to me, especially away from home.

To Second Division

Despite Blissett's great scoring efforts away from home, Brentford sorely missed Dean Holdsworth. It has been proved time and again that you cannot sell top strikers and get away with it. A lack of drawn games eventually sealed Brentford's fate, and they will be hoping they don't spend another twenty odds years in the second division (the old third) like they did before winning promotion.

Cambridge struggled to find the net last year, and it is impossible to forecast how they might do this time around. They haven't been around long enough to evaluate the form of years gone by in different divisions, so we shall have to wait and see before including their fixtures in our bets.

Only two teams in all the English leagues conceded more goals than Bristol Rovers (Chester and Preston), so the early results in the coming season should prove informative.

When they won the old third division in 1990, they did so by conceding only 35 goals in 46 games. Out of interest they were unbeaten at home, and drew a large number of games (15). These stats might just help when we have something to go on after the first few weeks of the season.

To Division Three

Chester will have to get their act together if they are not to plummet straight out of the league.

Any team conceding over one hundred league goals in a season must have serious problems, and scoring less than half that number doesn't help either!

It would be unusual for a team that has been relegated to be amongst the favourites to finish bottom of the next league down, but Chester must be on your short list. No fewer than twelve teams beat them twice last year.

They did well to score three goals away from home on three occasions last year, but in the process they conceded eleven goals and won only one point!

They let in 47 goals at home, and get ready to include Chester in some high scoring matches.

Preston managed to concede 94 goals, yet they look a better all round side and might just do the best of the four relegated sides. They won 13 games which is good for a relegated side, and provided they can tighten up that defence they could bounce straight back up.

Wigan and Mansfield both turned too many winning opportunities into draws and are probably best left alone until we get a glimpse of their form in the third division.

To Scottish Division One

Falkirk and Airdrie finished up having the same number of points at the bottom of the premier, yet they achieved them in totally different ways.

Falkirk won eleven and drew seven, whilst Airdrie won just six and drew seventeen.

Little wonder then that Falkirk are preferred in the betting to Airdrie, though both teams are closely priced in a group of four teams fancied to win the division.

Only one point separated the sides the season before (in Airdrie's favour) so it looks bound to be close again, albeit in a different division.

The last time the two teams were in this league they finished first and second separated once more by just a point, when Falkirk finished as champions

In a fiercely competitive league I will wait for some results before I put a one, two or 'x' beside a team in this division.

To Scottish Division Two

Cowdenbeath were the whipping boys of Scottish football last year, letting in an average of two and a half goals a game.

Generally quoted at around 10/1, I believe Cowdenbeath could be good value for the second division. They have come back down, straight after going up, but it should be remembered that they only just failed to gain promotion the year before. When they went up in 1992 they easily won the most games despite only finishing runners-up, so they could be good value as well on the weekly coupons.

Meadowbank are favourites or thereabouts to bounce back and they could well do so, but I see Cowdenbeath being much the best value of the two.

Pools Information

Where the draws occurred

League producing the most jackpot draws		League producing the most 0-0 draws:		League with the most higher scoring draws:	
1 Premier Divn	14.3%	1 First Divn	10.0%	1 Scottish Pmr	6.8%
2 Scottish Pmr	13.2%	2 Premier Divn	8.2%	1 Scottish Div. 1	6.8%
3 Third Divn	13.0%	3 Scottish Div. 2	8.0%	3 Second Divn	6.3%
4 Second Divn	12.1%	4 Second Divn	7.8%	3 Third Divn	6.3%
5 Scottish Div. 1	11.7%	5 Scottish Pmr	7.6%	5 First Divn	6.2%
6 Scottish Div. 2	10.6%	6 Scottish Div. 1	6.8%	5 Scottish Div.2	6.2%
7 First Division	10.5%	7 Third Divn	4.8%	7 Premier Divn	5.6%

Correct Score Draws-odds Table

This table actually shows the correct odds in terms of regularity of results last season.

For example, you can see at a glance that the 1-1 draw occurred once in every seven games in the Premier Division.

Keep an eye on this season's results, and then you can be sure of finding the true value of odds on offer.

	0-0	1-1	2-2	3-3
Premier Division	11/1	6/1	22/1	66/1
First Division	9/1	17/2	22/1	50/1
Second Division	12/1	7/1	18/1	100/1
Third Division	20/1	7/1	18/1	150/1
Scottish Premier	12/1	13/2	16/1	125/1
Scottish First	16/1	8/1	18/1	66/1
Scottish Second	11/1	17/2	18/1	125/1

PREMIER DIVISION

Teams playing in the most jackpot draw matches		Teams playing in the most 0-0 Draws		Teams that played in the most high scoring drawn matches	
Sheffield Weds	11	Blackburn	7	Coventry	5
Chelsea	8	Arsenal	6	Crystal Palace	5
Man. City	8	Ipswich	6	Middlesbro'	5
Aston Villa	7	Chelsea	5	Oldham	5
Crystal Palace	7	Aston Villa	4	Ipswich	4
Leeds	7	Crystal Palace	4	Leeds	4
Sheffield Utd	7	Leeds	4	Liverpool	3
Wimbledon	7	Manchester Utd	4	Everton	2
Ipswich	6	Q.P.R.	4	Man. Utd	2
Man. United	6	Southampton	4	Man. City	2
Nott'm Forest	6	Tottenham	4	Q.P.R.	2
Q.P.R.	6	Coventry	3	Sheffield Weds	2
Southampton	5	Everton	3	Southampton	2
Tottenham	5	Liverpool	3	Tottenham	2
Arsenal	5	Norwich	3	Wimbledon	2
Coventry	5	Nott'm Forest	3	Blackburn	1
Liverpool	5	Wimbledon	3	Chelsea	1
Middlesbro'	5	Man. City	2	Norwich	1
Norwich	5	Sheffield Utd	2	Nott'm Forest	1
Oldham	5	Middlesbro'	1	Sheffield Utd	1
Blackburn	3	Sheffield Weds	1	Arsenal	0
Everton	3	Oldham	0	Aston Villa	0

When we refer to higher scoring draws, we mean matches that ended in draw results at 2-2 or more.

FIRST DIVISION

Teams playing in the most jackpot draw matches		Teams playing in the most 0-0 Draws		Teams that played in the most high scoring drawn matches	
Southend	8	Luton	10	Cambridge	7
Peterborough	8	Bristol City	9	Luton	6
Millwall	7	Birmingham	6	Swindon	6
Oxford	7	Millwall	6	Notts. County	5
Cambridge	6	Watford	6	Bristol Rovers	4
Notts County	6	Brentford	5	Sunderland	4
Wolves	6	Charlton	5	Birmingham	3
Bristol Rovers	5	Leicester	5	Charlton	3
Charlton	5	Notts. County	5	Millwall	3
Derby	5	Sunderland	5	Oxford	3
Grimsby	5	Barnsley	4	Watford	3
Luton	5	Derby	4	Wolves	3
Portsmouth	5	Newcastle	4	Bristol City	2
Barnsley	4	Oxford	4	Newcastle	2
Brentford	4	Peterborough	4	Peterborough	2
Leicester	4	Swindon	4	Portsmouth	2
Tranmere	4	Tranmere	4	Southend	2
Watford	4	West Ham	4	Tranmere	2
West Ham	4	Wolves	4	West Ham	2
Birmingham	3	Cambridge	3	Barnsley	1
Bristol City	3	Portsmouth	3	Brentford	1
Newcastle	3	Southend	3	Grimsby	1
Swindon	3	Bristol Rovers	2	Leicester	1
Sunderland	2	Grimsby	1	Derby	0

SECOND DIVISION

Teams playing in the most jackpot draw matches		Teams playing in the most 0-0 Draws		Teams that played in the most high scoring drawn matches	
Burnley	11	Bournemouth	6	Blackpool	6
Bournemouth	10	Fulham	6	Exeter	6
Fulham	9	Plymouth	6	Stockport	6
Reading	9	Swansea	6	Preston	5
Stoke	8	Exeter	5	Bradford City	4
Rotherham	7	Hartlepool	5	Rotherham	4
Blackpool	6	Hull	5	West Brom	4
Bradford City	6	Stockport	5	Burnley	3
Brighton	6	Wigan	5	Hartlepool	3
Exeter	6	Leyton Orient	4	Mansfield	3
Bolton	5	Mansfield	4	Plymouth	3
Huddersfield	5	Reading	4	Port Vale	3
Hull	5	Blackpool	3	Swansea	3
Leyton Orient	5	Bradford City	3	Bolton	2
Port Vale	5	Port Vale	3	Brighton	2
Hartlepool	4	Rotherham	3	Chester	2
Mansfield	4	Bolton	2	Fulham	2
Stockport	4	Burnley	2	Huddersfield	2
Swansea	4	Huddersfield	2	Reading	2
West Brom	4	Stoke	2	Stoke	2
Wigan	4	West Brom	2	Wigan	2
Plymouth	3	Brighton	1	Hull	1
Chester	2	Chester	1	Bournemouth	0
Preston	2	Preston	1	Leyton Orient	0

THIRD DIVISION

Teams playing in the most jackpot draw matches		Teams playing in the most 0-0 Draws		Teams that played in the most high scoring drawn matches	
Hereford	12	Bury	5	Carlisle	6
Doncaster	10	Darlington	4	Scunthorpe	5
Gillingham	10	Scunthorpe	4	Torquay	5
Wrexham	9	Barnet	3	Northampton	4
Darlington	7	Chesterfield	3	Scarborough	4
Rochdale	7	York	3	Chesterfield	3
York	7	Carlisle	2	Darlington	3
Lincoln	6	Colchester	2	Rochdale	3
Shrewsbury	6	Doncaster	2	Shrewsbury	3
Barnet	5	Halifax	2	Barnet	2
Cardiff	5	Hereford	2	Bury	2
Chesterfield	5	Lincoln	2	Cardiff	2
Crewe	5	Northampton	2	Colchester	2
Halifax	5	Shrewsbury	2	Crewe	2
Scarborough	5	Wrexham	2	Doncaster	2
Walsall	4	Cardiff	1	Gillingham	2
Carlisle	3	Gillingham	1	Halifax	2
Scunthorpe	3	Torquay	1	Walsall	2
Bury	2	Walsall	1	York	2
Northampton	2	Crewe	0	Hereford	1
Colchester	1	Rochdale	0	Lincoln	1
Torquay	1	Scarborough	0	Wrexham	0

SCOTTISH PREMIER DIVISION

Teams playing in the most jackpot draw matches		Teams playing in the most 0-0 Draws		Teams that played in the most high scoring drawn matches	
St. Johnstone	12	Airdrie	5	Airdrie	5
Celtic	9	Hearts	5	Falkirk	5
Hearts	9	Hibernian	5	Hibernian	5
Airdrie	7	Motherwell	5	St. Johnstone	5
Partick	6	Dundee	4	Partick	4
Dundee	5	Dundee United	4	Aberdeen	3
Motherwell	5	Aberdeen	3	Dundee	3
Aberdeen	4	St. Johnstone	3	Motherwell	3
Dundee United	4	Celtic	2	Celtic	1
Rangers	4	Partick	2	Dundee United	1
Hibernian	3	Rangers	2	Rangers	1
Falkirk	2	Falkirk	0	Hearts	0

SCOTTISH DIVISION ONE

Raith	9	Ayr	6	Clydebank	5
Ayr	9	Hamilton	5	Morton	4
Kilmarnock	8	Stirling	4	Ayr	3
Meadowbank	6	St. Mirren	4	Cowdenbeath	3
Stirling	6	Clydebank	3	Dumbarton	3
Clydebank	5	Dumbarton	3	Hamilton	3
Hamilton	4	Dunfermline	3	Kilmarnock	3
Morton	4	Raith	3	Meadowbank	3
St. Mirren	4	Morton	2	Raith	3
Cowdenbeath	3	Cowdenbeath	1	Stirling	3
Dunfermline	3	Kilmarnock	1	Dunfermline	2
Dumbarton	1	Meadowbank	1	St. Mirren	1

SCOTTISH DIVISION TWO

Teams playing in the most jackpot draw matches		Teams playing in the most 0-0 Draws		Teams that played in the most high scoring drawn matches	
Stranraer	8	Arbroath	5	Alloa	5
Albion	7	East Stirling	5	East Fife	5
Clyde	6	Stenhousemuir	5	Queen's Park	5
Alloa	5	Brechin	5	East Stirling	3
Forfar	5	Montrose	4	Q'n of the S'th	3
Queen's Park	5	Stranraer	4	Stranraer	3
Berwick	4	Clyde	3	Albion	2
East Fife	4	Forfar	3	Forfar	2
Q'n of the S'th	4	Alloa	2	Stenhousemuir	2
Arbroath	3	Berwick	2	Berwick	1
Stenhousemuir	3	Q'n of the S'th	2	Brechin	1
Montrose	2	Queen's Park	2	Clyde	1
Brechin	1	Albion	1	Montrose	1
Eat Stirling	1	East Fife	1	Arbroath	-

ROUND UP

Teams who played in most 1–1 draws		Teams who played in most 0-0 Draws		Teams who played in most higher scoring draws	
Hereford	12			Cambridge	7
St. Johnstone	12			Luton	6
Sheffield Wed.	11	Luton	10	Swindon	6
Burnley	11	Bristol City	9	Blackpool	6
Bournemouth	10	Blackburn	7	Carlisle	6
Doncaster	10			Exeter	6
Gillingham	10			Stockport	6

Teams who played in the least 1–1 draws		Teams who played in the least 0-0 Draws			
Colchester	1	Oldham	0	East Fife	1
Torquay	1	Crewe	0	Kilmarnock	1
Dumbarton	1	Rochdale	0	Albion	1
Brechin	1	Scarborough	0		
East Stirling	1	Falkirk	0		
Sunderland	2	Middlesbrough	1		
Chester	2	Sheffield Wed.	1	Teams who did	
Preston	2	Grimsby	1	not play in any	
Bury	2	Brighton	1	high scoring draws	
Northampton	2	Chester	1	Arsenal	
Falkirk	2	Preston	1	Aston Villa	
Montrose	2	Cardiff	1	Derby	
		Gillingham	1	Bournemouth	
		Torquay	1	Leyton Orient	
		Walsall	1	Wrexham	
		Cowdenbeath	1	Hearts	
		Meadowbank	1	Arbroath	

Jackpot Draws: for pools clients and fixed odds punters alike

Teams that produced jackpot draws (1-1) since the introduction of the new points system. Figures in brackets denote home and away jackpot draws. (up to and including the end of 92-93 season)

Premier		First	
Sheffield Wednesday	5 (4-1)	Cambridge	3 (2-1)
Crystal Palace	4 (3-1)	Wolves	3 (1-2)
Manchester City	4 (3-1)	Bristol Rovers	3 (2-1)
Chelsea	4 (1-3)	Luton	3 (2-1)
Leeds	4 (2-2)	Peterborough	3 (3-0)
Nottingham Forest	3 (2-1)	Swindon	3 (1-2)
Sheffield United	3 (1-2)	Southend	2 (1-1)
Liverpool	3 (0-3)	Millwall	2 (1-1)
Wimbledon	3 (0-3)	Derby	2 (1-1)
Manchester United	2 (1-1)	Notts. County	2 (1-1)
Oldham	2 (2.0)	Oxford	2 (1-1)
Arsenal	2 (1-1)	Birmingham	1 (1-0)
Q.P.R.	2 (0-2)	Brentford	1 (1-0)
Tottenham	2 (1-1)	Portsmouth	1 (0-1)
Norwich	1 (1-0)	Sunderland	1 (0-1)
Blackburn	1 (1-0)	Watford	1 (0-1)
Ipswich	1 (1-0)	Bristol City	1 (0-1)
Aston Villa	1 (0-1)	Leicester	1 (0-1)
Coventry	Nil	Tranmere	1 (0-1)
Everton	Nil	Barnsley	Nil
Middlesbrough	Nil	Charlton	Nil
Southampton	Nil	Grimsby	Nil
		Newcastle	Nil
		West Ham	Nil

Jackpot Draws (continued)

Second		Third	
Fulham	5 (3-2)	Gillingham	4 (2-2)
Bournemouth	4 (2-2)	Darlington	4 (2-2)
Burnley	4 (1-3)	Crewe	4 (2-2)
Rotherham	4 (2-2)	Cardiff	3 (3-0)
Blackpool	3 (2-1)	Lincoln	3 (2-1)
Exeter	3 (2-1)	Wrexham	3 (1-2)
Stoke	3 (1-2)	Shrewsbury	3 (1-2)
Hull	2 (1-1)	Doncaster	3 (0-3)
Huddersfield	2 (2-0)	York	2 (1-1)
Leyton Orient	2 (1-1)	Chesterfield	2 (1-1)
Brighton	1 (1-0)	Hereford	2 (0-2)
Mansfield	1 (1-0)	Barnet	2 (1-1)
Stockport	1 (1-0)	Bury	1 (1-0)
Reading	1 (1-0)	Halifax	1 (1-0)
Hartlepool	1 (0-1)	Carlisle	1 (1-0)
Bradford	1 (0-1)	Walsall	1 (1-0)
Plymouth	1 (0-1)	Scarborough	1 (1-0)
Bolton	1 (0-1)	Rochdale	1 (0-1)
W.B.A.	1 (0-1)	Scunthorpe	1 (0-1)
Port Vale	1 (0-1)		

Scottish Premier

St. Johnstone	7 (3-4)
Airdrie	4 (2-2)
Dundee	3 (2-1)
Motherwell	2 (1-1)
Partick	2 (2-0)
Aberdeen	2 (1-1)
Hearts	2 (1-1)
Hibernian	1 (1-0)
Rangers	1 (0-1)
Falkirk	1 (0-1)
Celtic	1 (0-1)
Dundee United	Nil

Scottish First Division

Stirling	3 (1-2)
Ayr	3 (0-3)
Clydebank	2 (2-0)
Dunfermline	2 (1-1)
Kilmarnock	2 (1-1)
Raith	2 (0-2)
Hamilton	1 (1-0)
St. Mirren	1 (1-0)
Cowdenbeath	1 (1-0)
Meadowbank	1 (1-0)
Morton	1 (1-0)
Dumbarton	1 (0-1)

Scottish Second Division

Queen's Park	3 (2-1)
Stranraer	2 (1-1)
Alloa	2 (1-1)
Albion	2 (0-2)
Clyde	2 (0-2)
Montrose	1 (1-0)
East Fife	1 (1-0)
Berwick	1 (1-0)
Forfar	1 (1-0)
Queen of the South	1 (0-1)
Arbroath	Nil
Brechin	Nil
East Stirling	Nil
Stenhousemuir	Nil

265

Did you know . . .

This sector takes a look at some of the more unknown details of each team in their respective leagues last year.

This could be the chance for you to win a pint or two down at your local watering hole.

I have hosted football trivia evenings in pubs and clubs, and you might like to use some of this information to set up a quiz night. You will find that landlords are quite generous with the free ale if you are able to pull in another twenty or thirty people on a quiet Monday night because of your quiz.

Some of the more extreme facts are listed below, and on the following pages you will find comment on the English and Scottish clubs in divisional order.

Did you know . . .

That **Arsenal** averaged a goal every 118 minutes in the second half of their home matches last season.

That **Oldham** were the only Premier team not to be losing at home at half time. (Useful double-result information).

That **Nottingham Forest** were the only Premier team not to surrender a half time lead all season.

That **Liverpool** lost their opening match of the season for the first time in eleven years. (Sign of things to come).

That **Arsenal** lost more games than Crystal Palace last season. (Yet they finished ten places higher in the league).

That **Oldham** took until the ninth of January to win an away game.

That **Niall Quinn** of Manchester City was the first player ever to be sent off in the new Premier Division.

That **Liverpool's** 5-1 defeat at Coventry was their heaviest in over 15 years.

Did you know ... Premier Division

Arsenal   were drawing at half time in seven of their home matches, but did not win any of them.

Aston Villa   lost at their shortest price of the season both home and away. They lost to Oldham at home when 2/5 chances, and went down 1-2 at Q. P.R. when starting at even money

Blackburn   scored the first goal of the match in 27 of their 42 league games.

Chelsea   started at 2/1 or less in nine of their away games, yet won only one of them (Everton) when they were 9/5.

Coventry   lost all six matches at home when they were behind at half time.

Crystal Palace were the last team to win a match at the start of the season.

Everton   didn't win at their two shortest prices when playing at home (4/6 & 8/11) but did win when starting at their biggest price which was 9/4 against Liverpool.

Ipswich   lost both matches when they started 8/13 at home (shortest price of the season) against Middlesbrough and Oldham, but they beat Manchester United at biggest price of 2/1

Leeds   conceded four goals away from home five times, at Middlesbro', Ipswich, Manchester City, Tottenham and Norwich.

Liverpool   failed to win in their four shortest priced away fixtures at 6/5 and 11/8 three times. They won at their biggest price though which was 3/1 at Arsenal.

Manchester City	were the only side to be beaten twice by Middlesbrough.
Manchester Utd.	suffered their heaviest defeat of the season (0-3 to Everton) in their very first home game.
Middlesbrough	started at 2/1 or less five times on their travels without winning.
Norwich	started at 6/4 five times away from home and lost all of them at an aggregate score of 3-17.
Nottingham Frst	were the only team to beat Leeds at Elland Road (4-1).
Oldham	pulled off a near 20/1 treble in escaping relegation, by winning their last three games of the season. It was the only time they won three games in a row.
Q.P.R	were drawing in fourteen matches at half-time, but only won two of them.
Sheffield United	lost five home games, and lost to all five teams again in the corresponding away fixtures.
Sheffield Wed.	were either winning or losing in eighteen of their matches at home at half-time. They were drawing in only three and failed to win any of them.
Southampton	started at 5/4 in three home games and won them all by a single goal.
Tottenham	did not win in any of their five shortest priced efforts away from home and lost four of them.
Wimbledon	were the only team to score more than two goals at Liverpool when they won 3-2.

Did you know . . . First Division

Barnsley   led in fourteen matches at half-time and won thirteen of them.

Birmingham   were the only side beaten twice by Bristol City.

Brentford   were the only side beaten twice by Cambridge.

Bristol City   conceded eighteen goals more than they scored despite finishing seven places above the relegation zone.

Bristol Rovers   achieved 'the double' over Millwall at odds of over 12/1.

Cambridge   were drawing at half-time in eighteen games and won just two.

Charlton   led in just nine games at half-time but won eight of them and drew the other.

Derby   started at 13/8 on four occasions away from home and did not win any of the matches.

Grimsby   drew only seven games, the least in the division.

Leicester   only started odds on once away from home, when they lost 0-3 at Peterborough.

Luton   drew 21 of their matches which was five more than any other team in the division.

Millwall   were leading at half time in 11 of their 14 home victories.

Newcastle   did not win at either of their two shortest priced efforts on their travels. They drew at both Luton (8/11) and Southend (4/5).

Notts County   started at less than 2/1 seven times away from home without winning.

Oxford	were the only team to be beaten twice by Brentford.
Peterborough	were the only team to be beaten twice by Notts County.
Portsmouth	scored the first goal of the game in 29 of their 46 matches.
Southend	started at less than 11/4 seven times away from home without winning.
Sunderland	did not win in their four shortest priced home performances between odds of 4/5 and 4/6.
Swindon	were 1-4 down at Birmingham before staging a remarkable comeback by winning 6-4.
Tranmere	were one of only two teams to beat Wolves twice, Derby were the other.
Watford	won only five points from a possible thirty nine when they were behind at half-time.
West Ham	won 17 of the 19 games they led in at half-time. They drew the other two games.
Wolves	started as hot favourites at 8/11 in six home matches but won only two of them against Peterborough and Birmingham.

Did you know . . . Second Division

Blackpool	won at their biggest price of the season, 9/1 at Stoke.
Bolton	scored five goals in the second half in two of their home games, winning both by five goals to nil i.e. they hadn't scored in either game in the opening forty five minutes.
Bournemouth	one of only two clubs who failed to score against Chester at home. The other team was Huddersfield.

Bradford	scored three goals at home on six occasions.
Brighton	won all twelve matches where they led at half-time.
Burnley	won at the five shortest prices they started at between 4/6 and 1/2 by a goals aggregate of 13-1.
Chester	were beaten twice by no less than twelve teams.
Exeter	were involved in eight matches at home which were decided by one goal. They lost seven of them, the only victory coming against Leyton Orient by one goal to nil.
Fulham	only conceded more than three goals at home once and that was after they took the lead against Bolton.
Hartlepool	lost by two goals or more fourteen times.
Huddersfield	conceded a goal in the first minute of the season. The only other club to do so was Colchester in the third division.
Hull	conceded three goals in nine minutes at Chester!
Leyton Orient	won more games than two of the teams who finished above them in the play-off positions.
Mansfield	were three goals up at home to Swansea in 26 minutes, but could only draw 3-3.
Plymouth	scored only 21 away goals but managed five at West Brom who ended up being promoted.
Port Vale	won fourteen of the twenty five matches they were drawing in at half-time.
Preston	conceded the second highest number of goals in England

Reading	started at 11/8 six times during the 'home season' and won five of them against Rotherham, Fulham, Plymouth, Brighton and Swansea.
Rotherham	scored exactly the same number of goals as they conceded which was sixty.
Stockport	won eleven home games, and had a two goal or more winning margin in ten of them. The only game they won by the odd goal was in their opening fixture against Burnley.
Stoke	beat seven teams both home and away, and were never beaten by the same team twice.
Swansea	lost just five games from the twenty they were drawing in at the interval.
West Brom	led at Stockport by scoring in the forty second minute. They went on to be beaten by five goals to one.
Wigan	scored a near sixteen to one 'double' over Leyton Orient.

Did you know . . . Third Division

Barnet	were the only team to beat Wrexham twice.
Bury	were losing in twelve of their matches at half-time and lost ten of them.
Cardiff	won all eight matches away from home where they started at 11/8 or shorter. (Ranged from 11/8 to 8/13)
Carlisle	found themselves 6-0 down at Bury by half-time, though they did not concede any more goals after the interval.
Chesterfield	were losing at home on four occasions by the interval, and they lost all four games.

Colchester	drew only five of their forty two matches.
Crewe	won all three matches away from home where they started as warm favourites. They won twice at 11/8 and were 5/4 when they won at Hereford.
Darlington	were the only team to be beaten twice by Halifax!
Doncaster	were involved in 21 matches which were decided by just a difference of one goal. They won ten of them and lost eleven.
Gillingham	won nine matches at home but none on their travels.
Halifax	were on level terms at half-time in fifteen matches and failed to win any, drawing four and losing eleven.
Hereford	took part in twelve jackpot draw games (1-1), with eight in front of their home fans and four away.
Lincoln	featured in twelve matches that finished with a scoreline of 2-1. They won seven of those games and lost five.
Northampton	were drawing in nineteen of their games at half-time and only won three of them.
Rochdale	were the only team to be beaten twice by Northampton.
Scarborough	drew one third of their home matches by the score of either 1-1 or 2-2.
Scunthorpe	won six matches away from home, but failed to beat any of those teams in front of their own fans.
Shrewsbury	were involved in twenty one matches where the result was decided by the difference of one goal.

Torquay	played in only one jackpot draw game all season (at home to Wrexham).
Walsall	finished fifth in the league but conceded 61 goals. There were eight teams which finished behind them who conceded less.
Wrexham	lost eight games in the whole season and they were behind at the interval in every one of them.
York	were the only side to beat Barnet twice.

Did you know . . . Scottish Premier Division

Aberdeen	won 16 games by two goals or more and 'only' finished nine points adrift of Rangers' record breaking season.
Airdrie	only managed to score 35 goals in 44 matches which made relegation inevitable.
Celtic	suffered through their attack which mustered 68 goals. Whilst that number might sound reasonable, it is worth noting that Aberdeen (who finished just four points ahead of Celtic) scored 87, and their arch rivals Rangers managed 97.
Dundee	lost all four matches against Celtic which you might expect, but they also failed to get a point against Partick Thistle.
Dundee United	beat Partick in all four matches with a goal aggregate of ten against two.
Falkirk	might have been a shade unfortunate to go down as they lost fourteen matches by just one goal.
Hearts	scored just 46 goals which might be a lowly record for a team which finished fifth in the division.

Hibernian	lost all four matches against Aberdeen scoring just two goals in the process and conceding ten.
Motherwell	lost twenty matches, losing half by a single goal and the other ten matches by two goals or more.
Partick	scored eleven goals in four matches against Dundee securing all eight points in the process.
Rangers	conceded more than two goals to just three teams during the season. They were the unlikely trio of Dundee, Hibernian and Partick.
St. Johnstone	drew twenty matches which was six more than Hearts who were next best with fourteen draws to their credit. For the record, Rangers and Falkirk drew the least games (7).

Did you know . . . Scottish First Division

Ayr United	drew the most matches which numbered eighteen, and half of those ended as jackpot draws (1-1). They drew no less than seven matches away from home 1-1.
Clydebank	won by four goals to one on three occasions at home. The last one being against champions Raith Rovers.
Cowdenbeath	won at their biggest price of the season (14/1), whilst they failed to win at home in 22 attempts.
Dumbarton	started at 7/2 or more eight times without winning. They lost five of those matches.
Dunfermline	featured in 24 matches that were either won or lost by a difference of just one goal.

Hamilton   started at 9/4 or more seven times without winning. They lost five of those matches.

Kilmarnock   took just one point from Dunfermline in four games. Form such as that looks a little suspect for the coming season with 'the big boys'.

Meadowbank   started at 2/1 or more in six home matches without winning any of them.

Morton   were consistent in conceding two goals in their away matches. They let two goals in on eight occasions and managed just one win whilst doing so.

Raith   had at least one thing in common with the mighty Glasgow Rangers. They lost just four matches all season. In those matches however, they were on the wrong end of a 2-12 goal aggregate.

Stirling   conceded one goal in a game on nineteen occasions, losing seven times whilst doing so.

St. Mirren   won fourteen matches by the difference of just a single goal.

Did you know . . . Scottish Second Division

Albion   lost by two goals or more fourteen times, and scored just 36 goals in 39 games.

Alloa   drew all three of their matches with Forfar 1-1.

Arbroath   won more matches away from home than they did in front of their own supporters.

Berwick   were involved in twenty four matches that were either won or lost by two goals or more.

Brechin had to thank their defence for a good season. They leaked just 32 goals in their 39 games.

Clyde lost all three of their matches against Brechin, and lost both games at home where they started at odds against.

East Fife scored plenty of goals yet finished only ninth in the league. Only two teams managed more goals finishing first and fourth.

East Stirling conceded 11 more goals than the two promoted clubs added together.

Forfar started at odds against twice at home and lost both matches.

Montrose lost seventeen matches by two goals or more, and won just five by that amount.

Queen o' t' Sth took only one point from a possible six against five of their rival clubs. They were Alloa, Brechin, Stenhousemuir, Arbroath and Forfar.

Queen's Park started between 6/4 and 5/1 on sixteen occasions away from home. They failed to win any of them.

Stenhousemuir won nine games at home, winning eight of them by two goals or more. The odd occasion was when they beat Queen of the South by two goals to one.

Stranraer drew the largest number of games in the division (15). You could argue that this statistic cost them a promotion place.

FIXED ODDS FOOTBALL BETTING

The Newsletter

FREE TRIAL OFFER

Although the material found in Win at Fixed Odds Football Betting has proven invaluable to users during the early part of the season it is important that you keep abreast of all the latest trends to maximise your potential profits. For instance did you know that we said that Norwich were the team to back to win 3-2 away from home - they won their first away match of the season 3-2 - *at odds of 100/1!*

More early season information that would have netted a tidy profit included:

- Rotherham's had a habit of 3-3 draws last year. First match of season drawn 3-3 at odds of 66/1!

- Leave Everton out of Pools selections we advised - 10 matches into the season and still no draws!

- Look for Darlington to be involved in jackpot draws we suggested - Darlington drew 3 of their first 5 matches 1-1!

- Man Utd consistently won 3-0 at home last season - in no time at all they won 3-0 twice at home this season!

- Teddy Sheringham was clearly superior to his colleagues in the first goal department in the 92/93 season - He scored the first goal of the game in Spurs first match of the season!

Convinced you need our newsletter? We are so sure that you will want the information we can provide that we will send you an up to date sample newsletter at ABSOLUTELY NO COST! When you choose to subscribe the rates are £10 for a single fortnightly issue, £25 for 4 issues and £69 for 13 issues. Cheques or P.O.'s should be payable to Oldcastle Books Ltd - we accept Access, Visa or Switch.

Please send your address details on a separate piece of paper to *Fixed Odds Newsletter, Oldcastle Books, 18 Coleswood Rd, Harpenden, Herts, AL5 1EQ* and we will send you the current newsletter by return post - Free of charge.